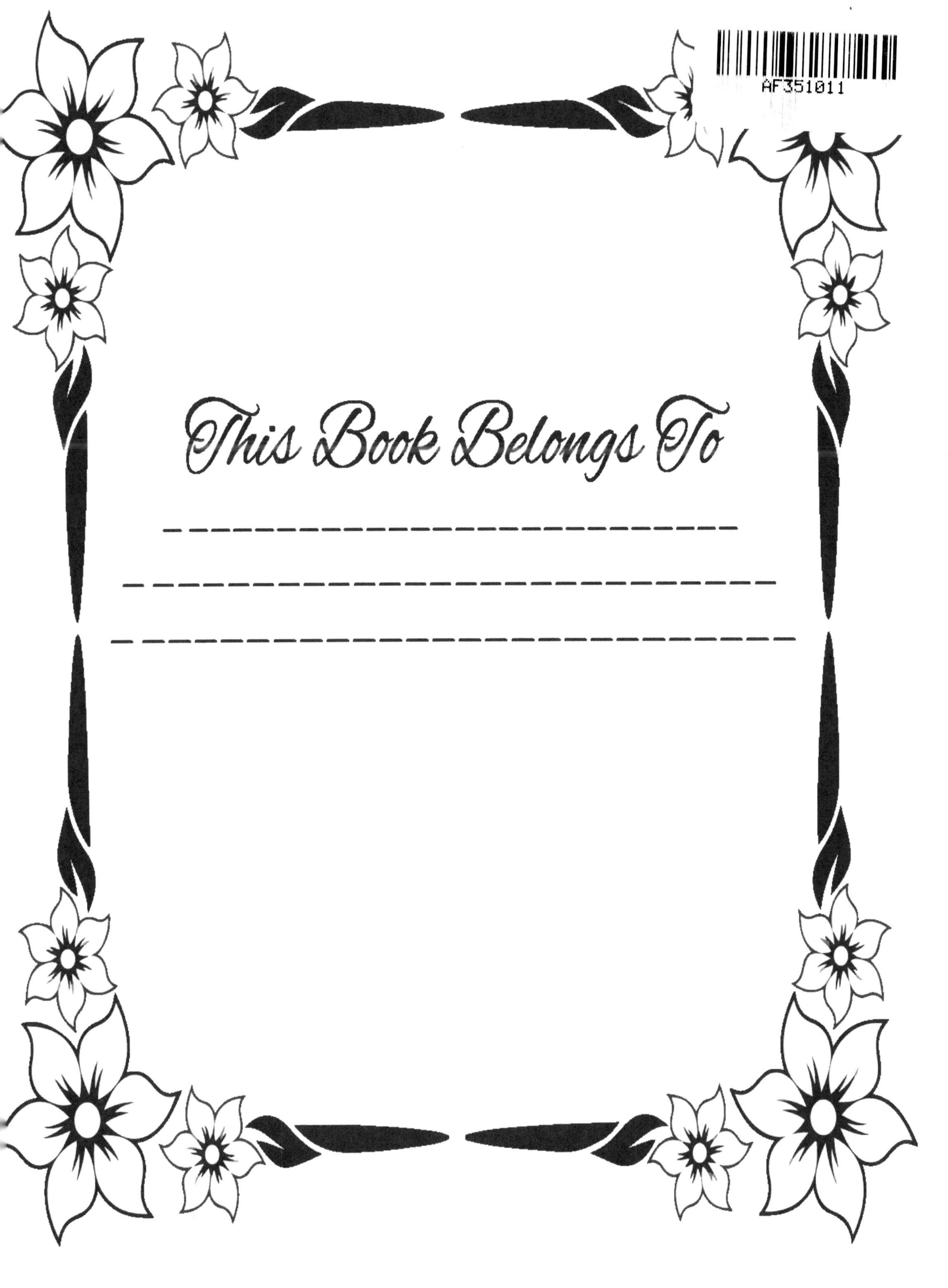

This Book Belongs To

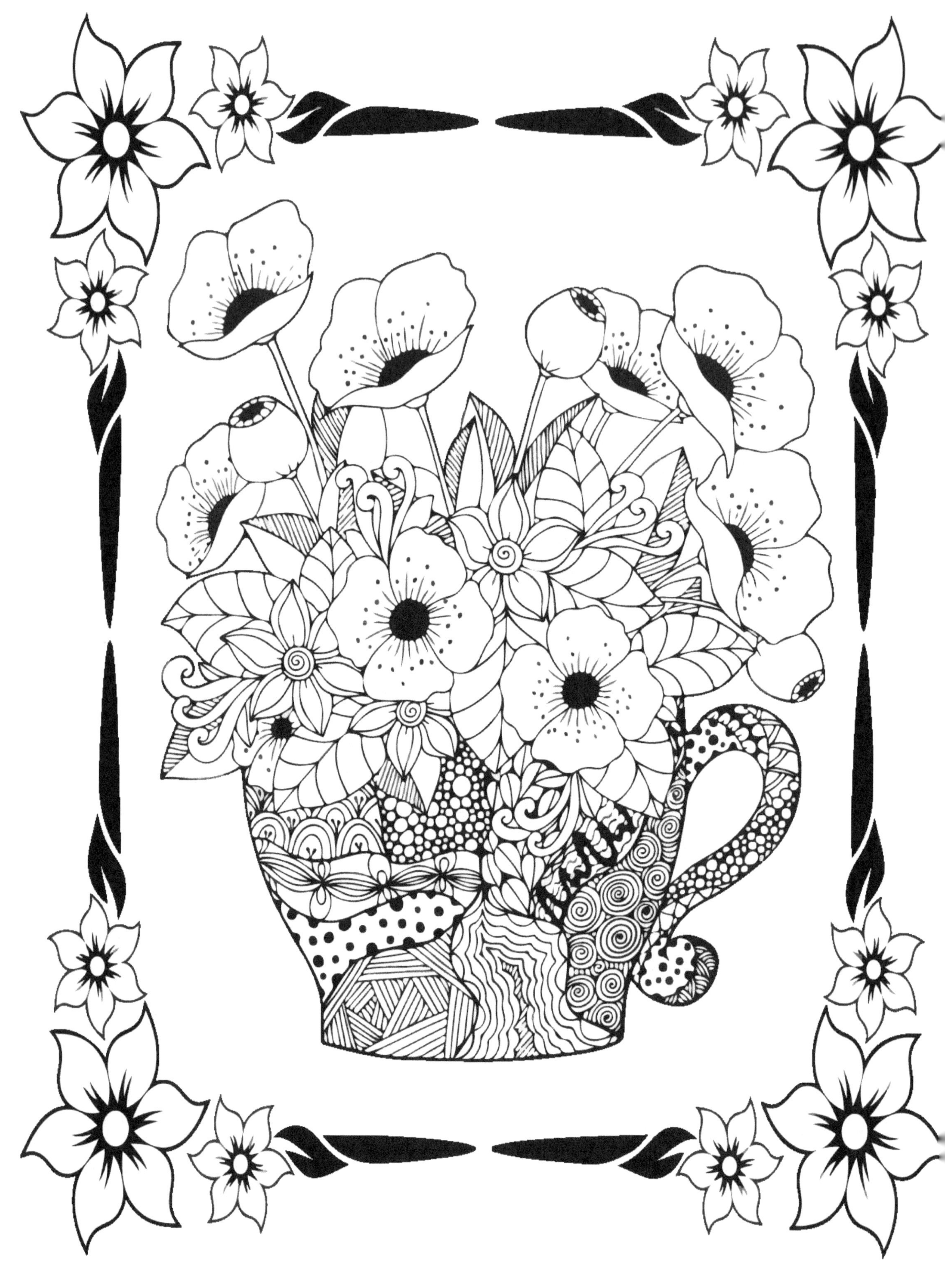

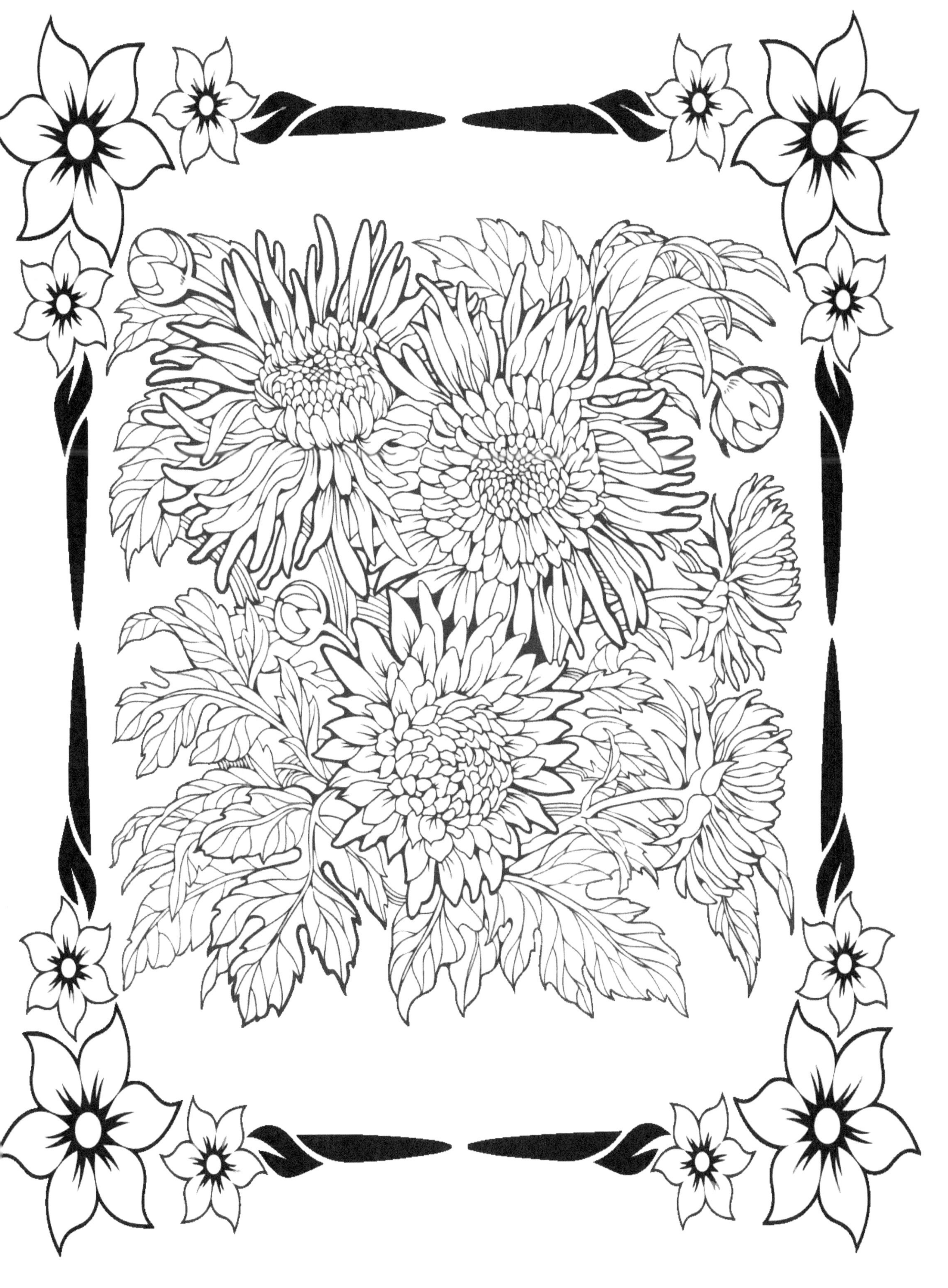

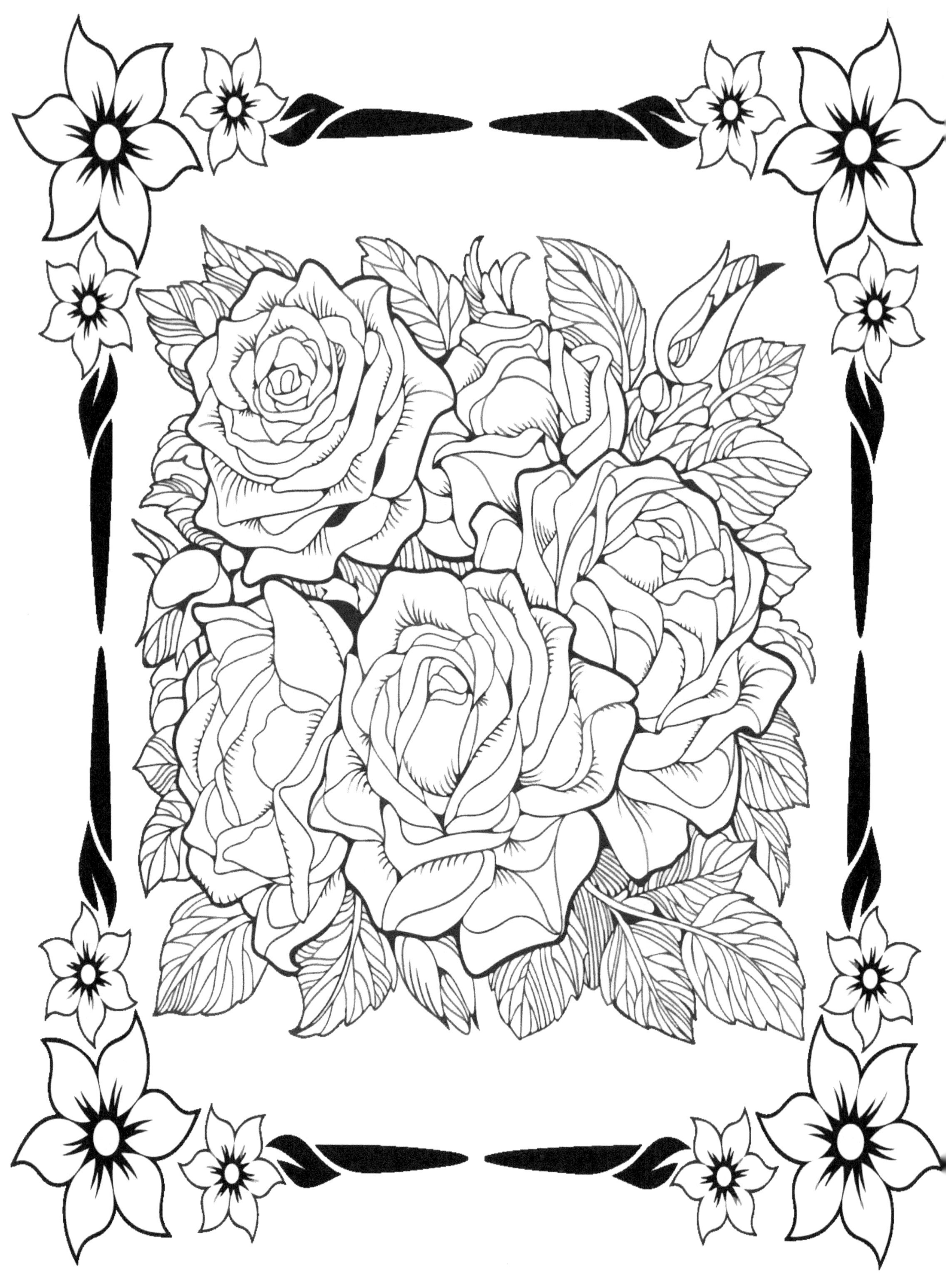

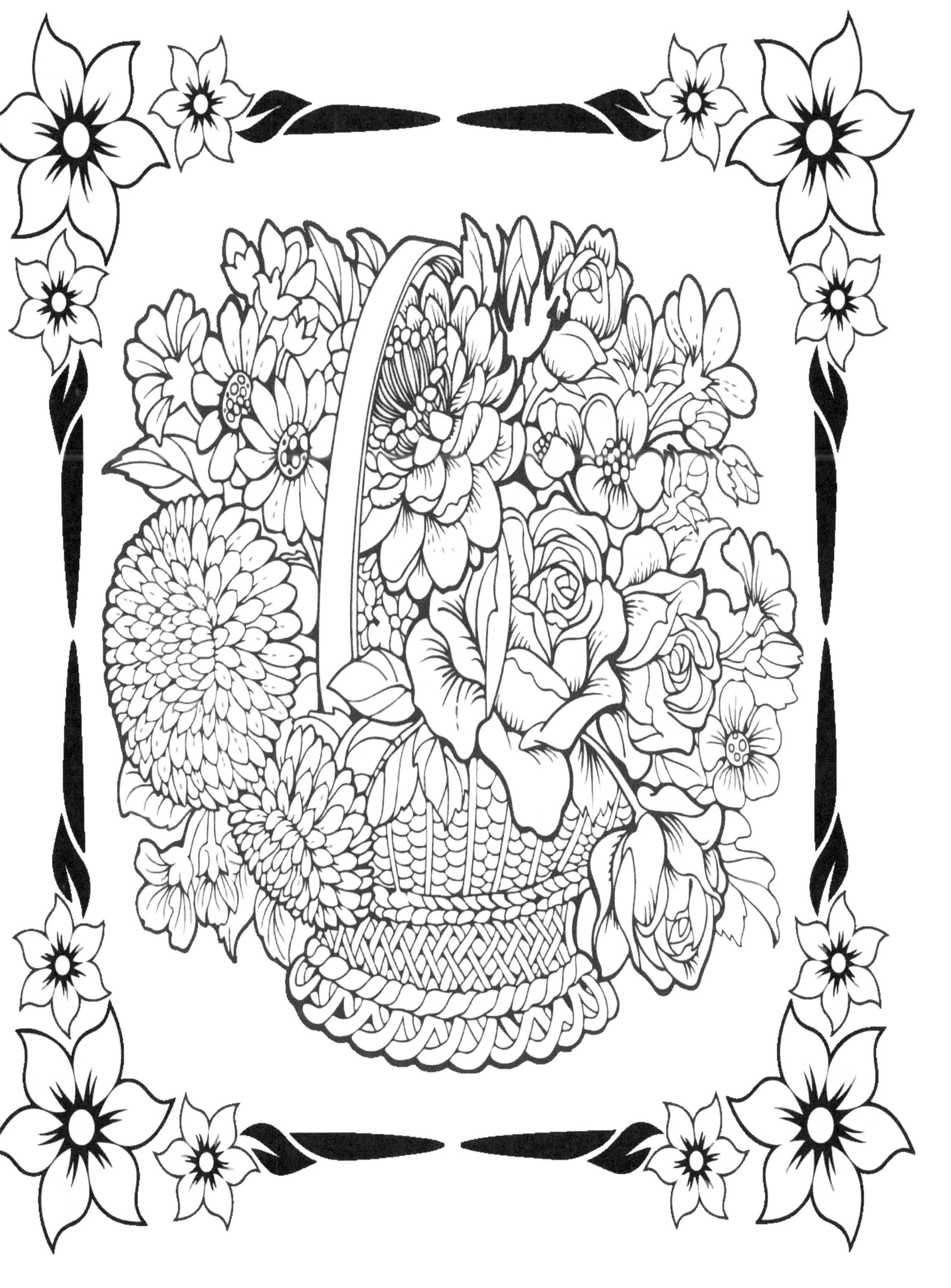

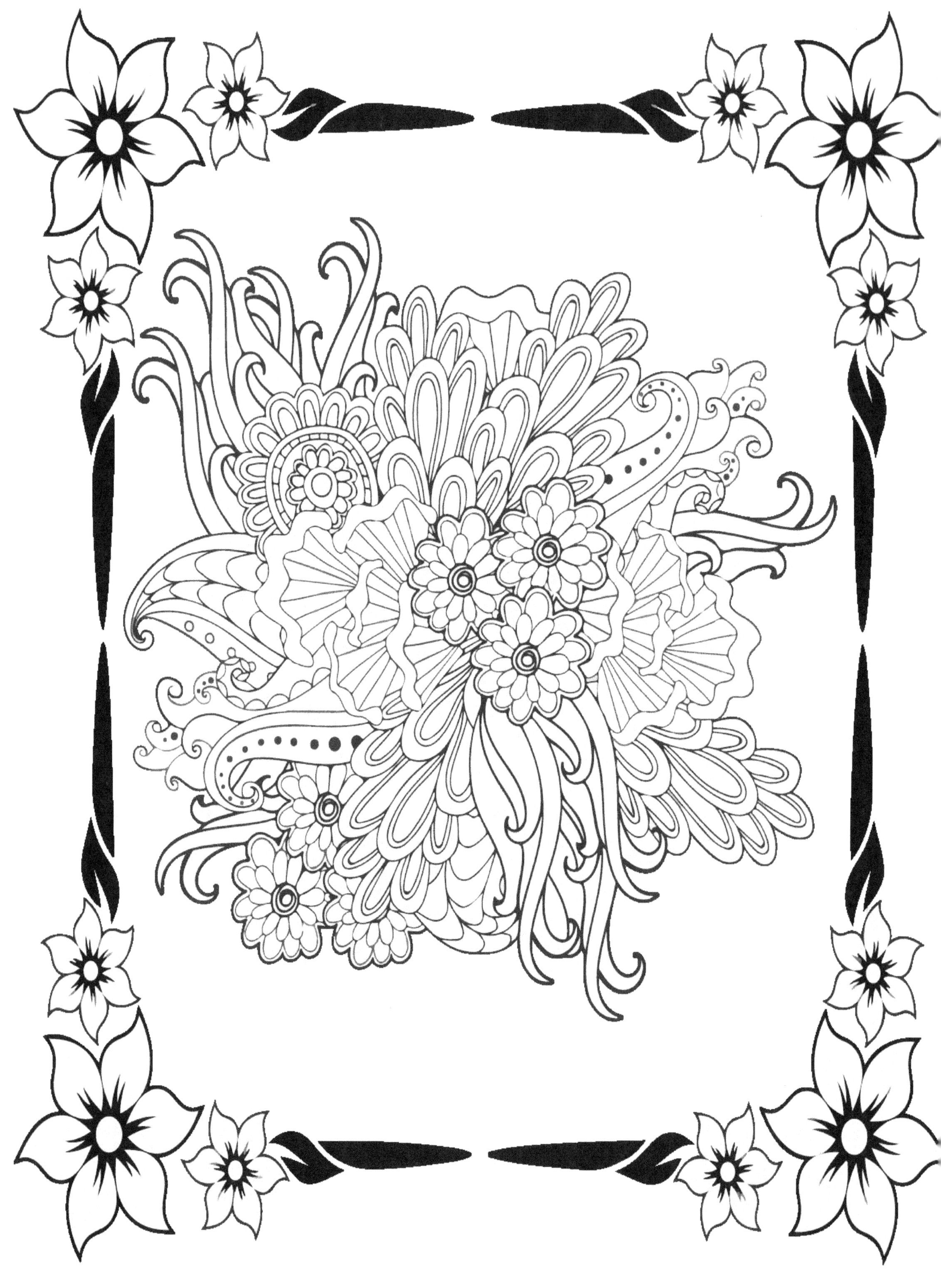

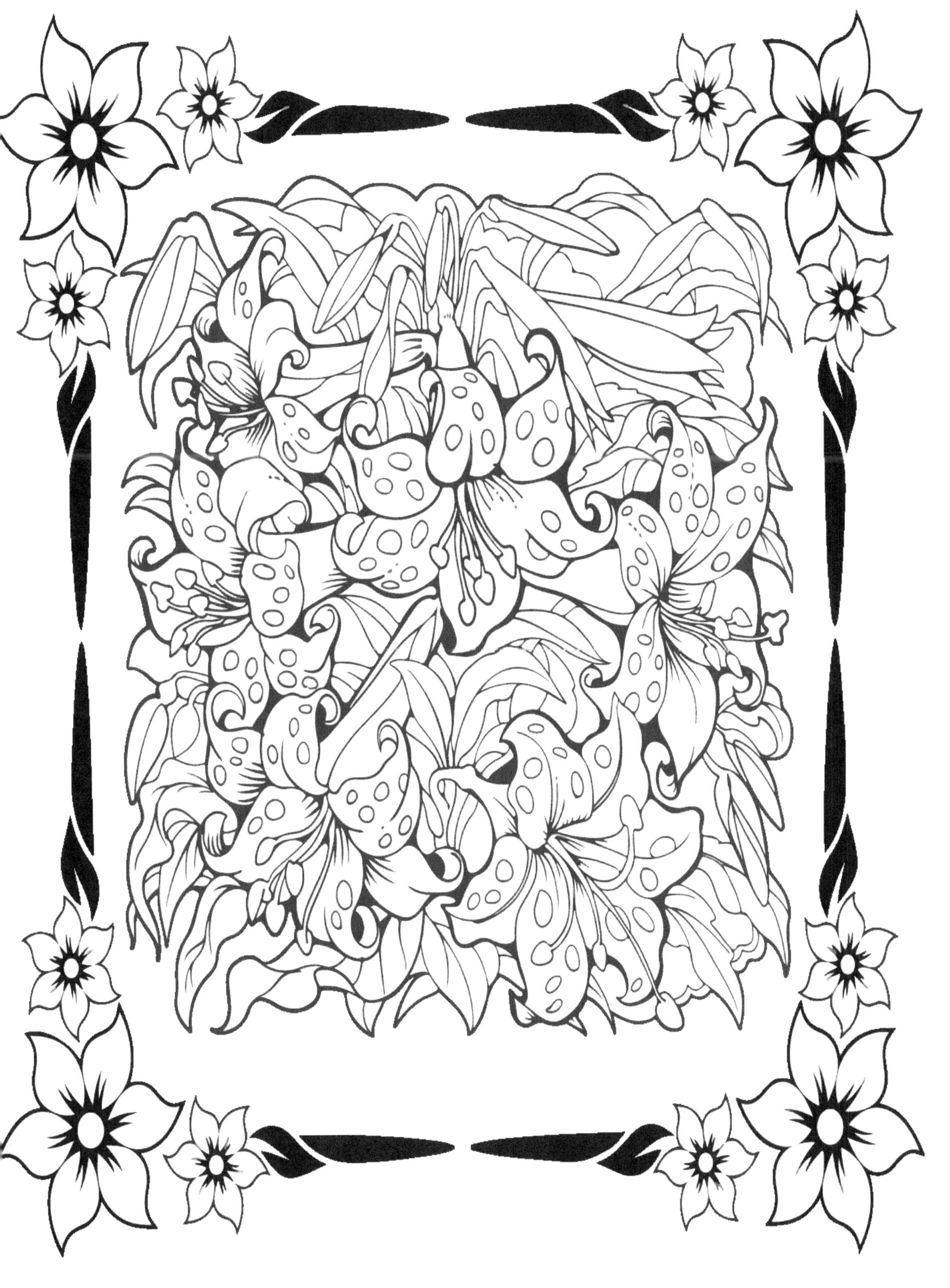

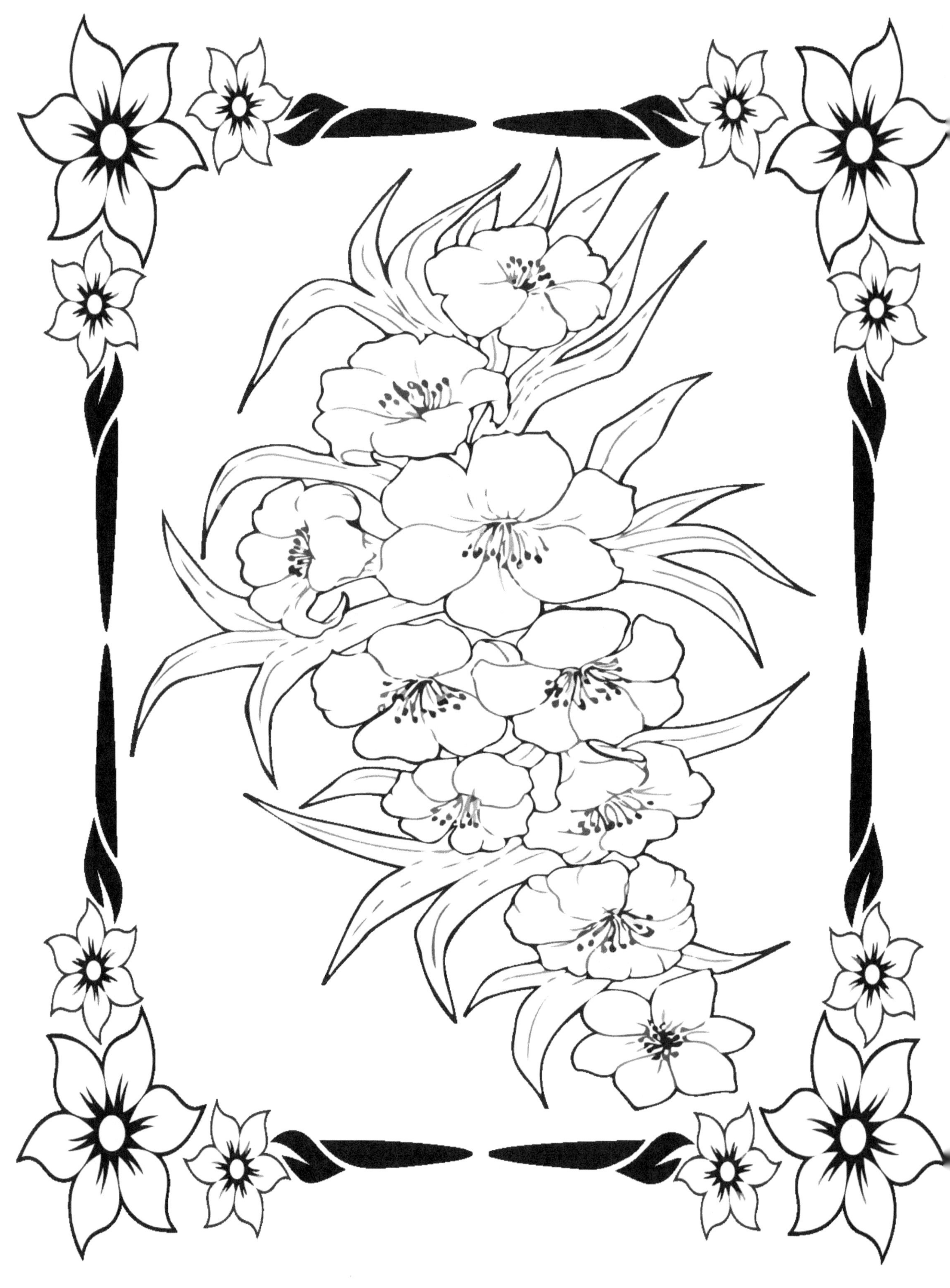

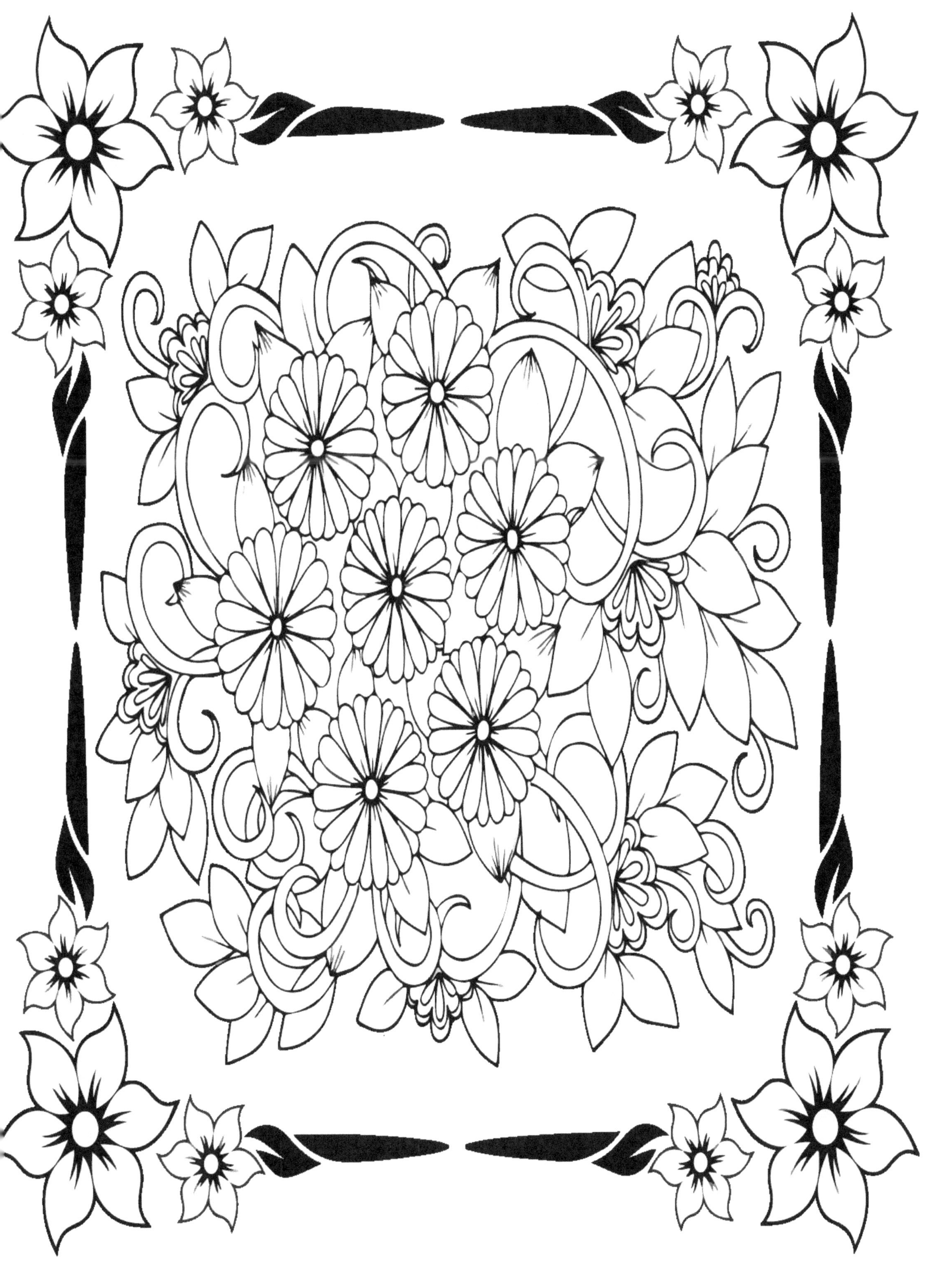

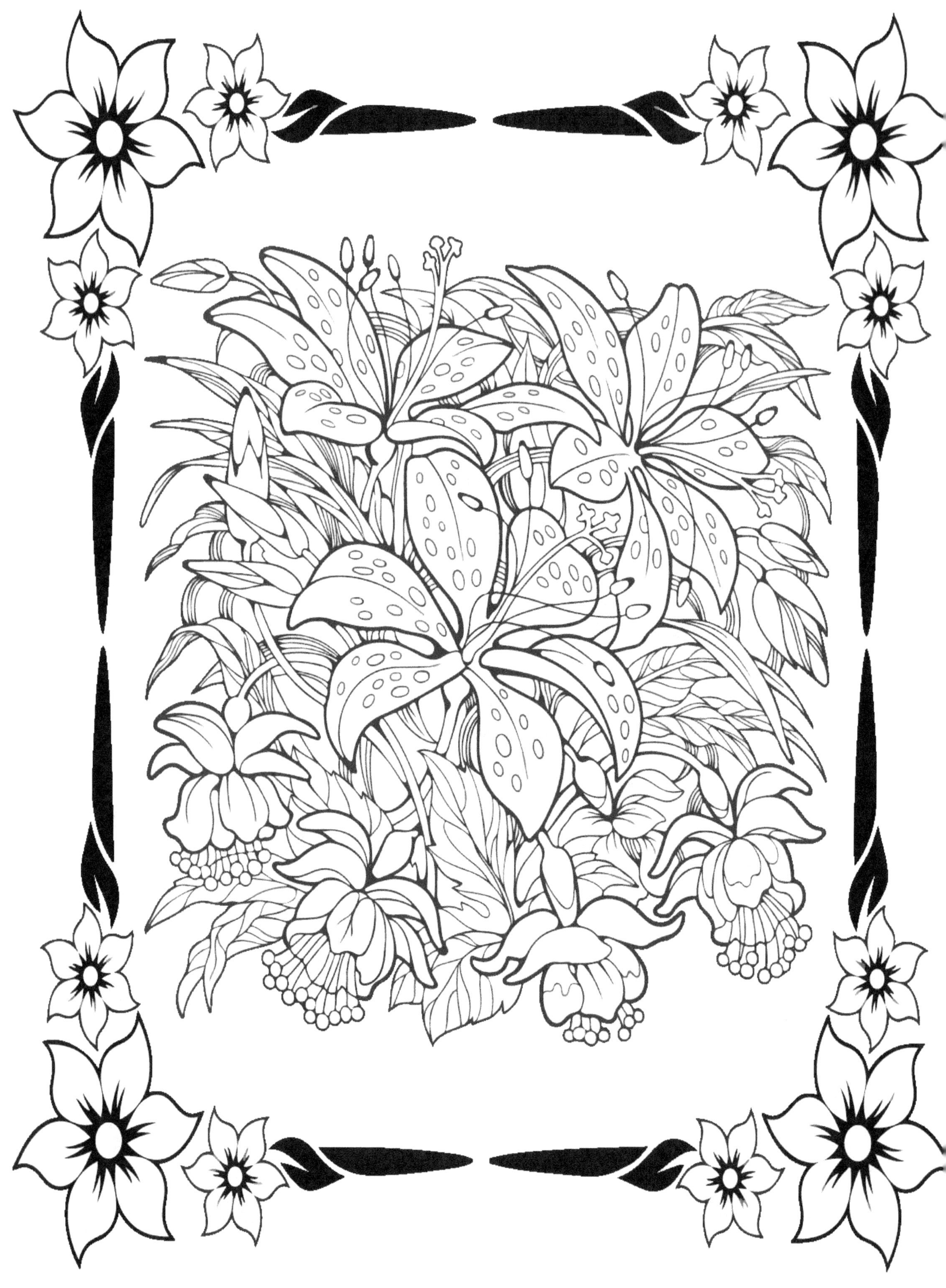

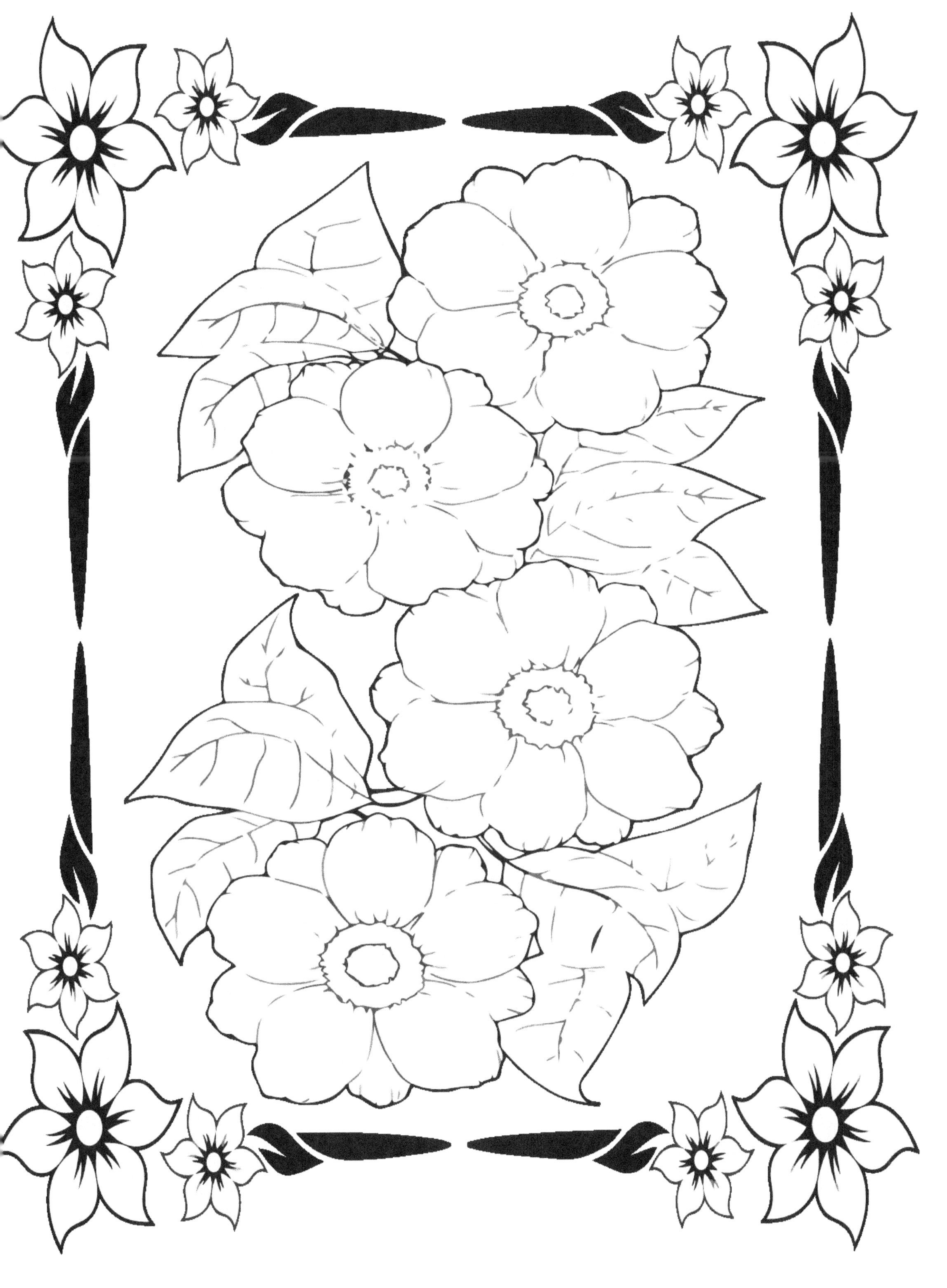

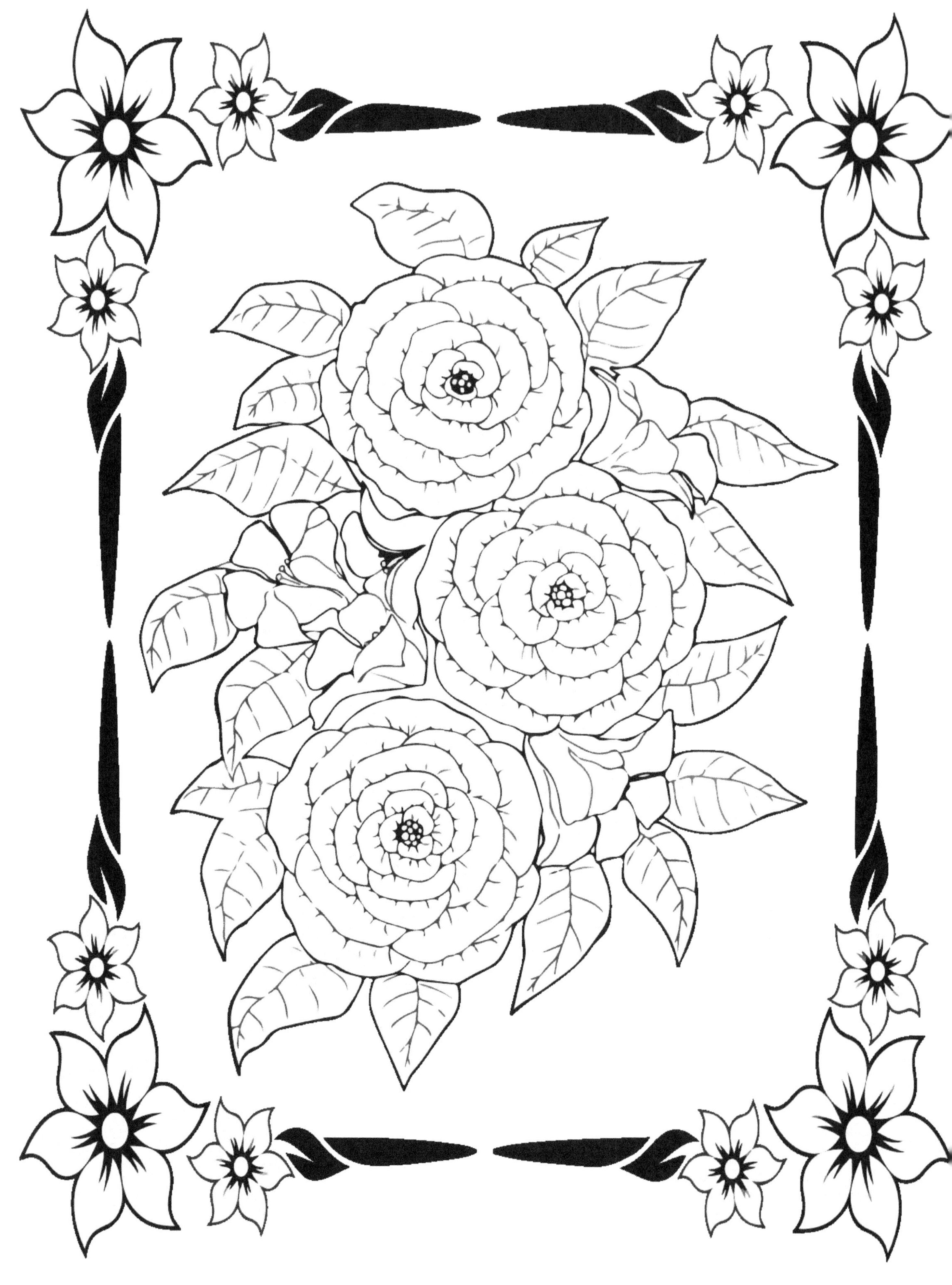

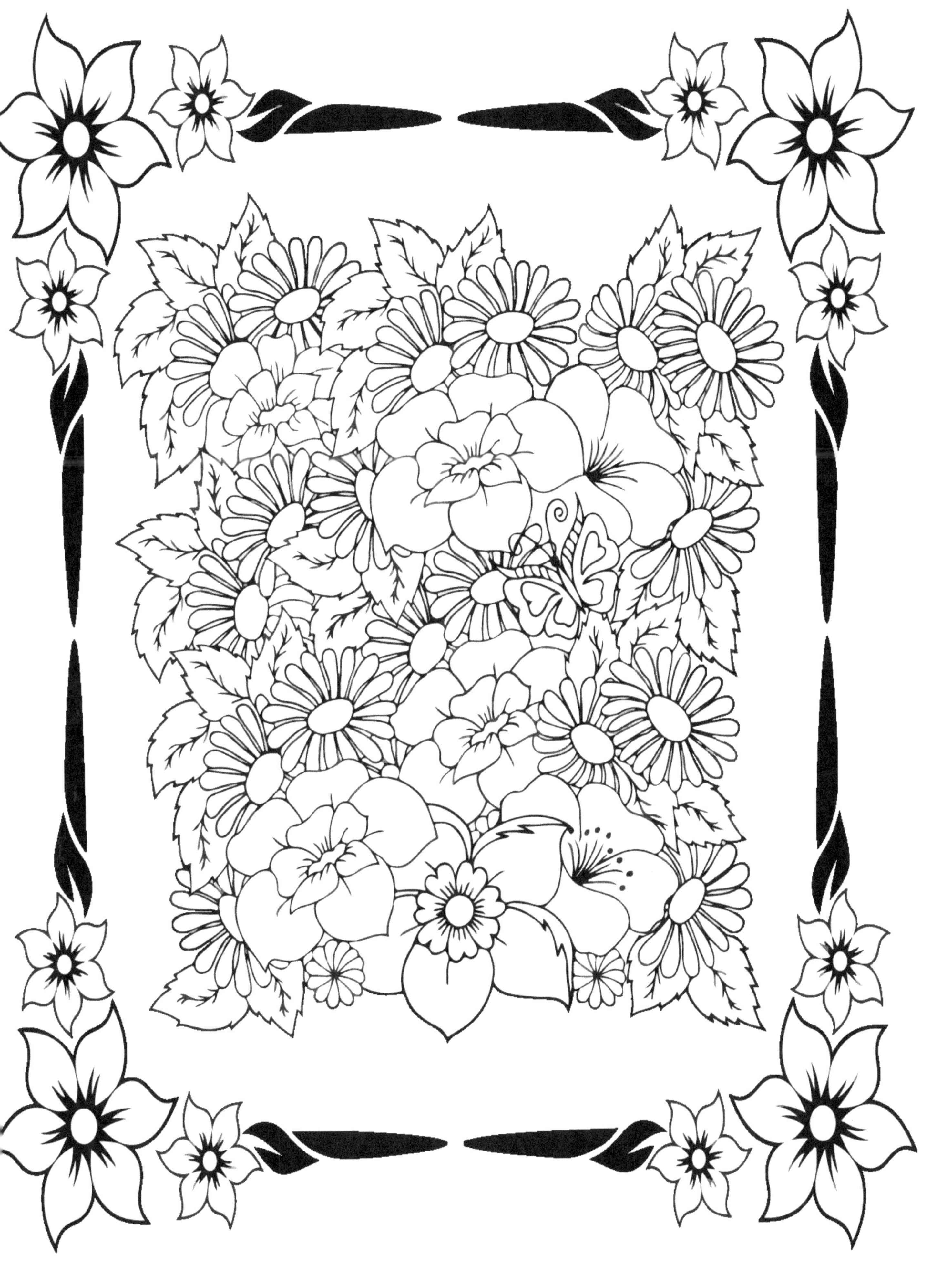

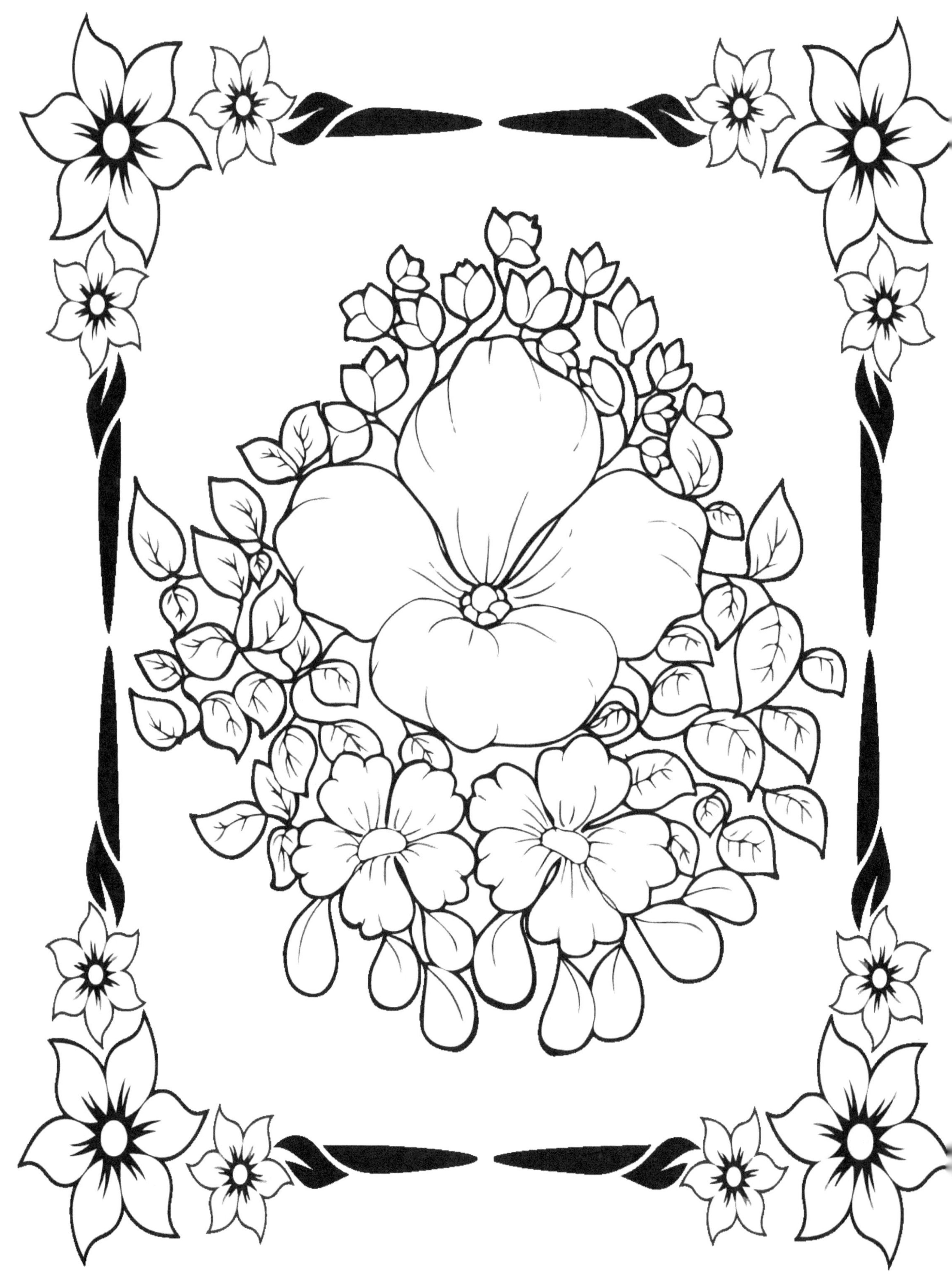

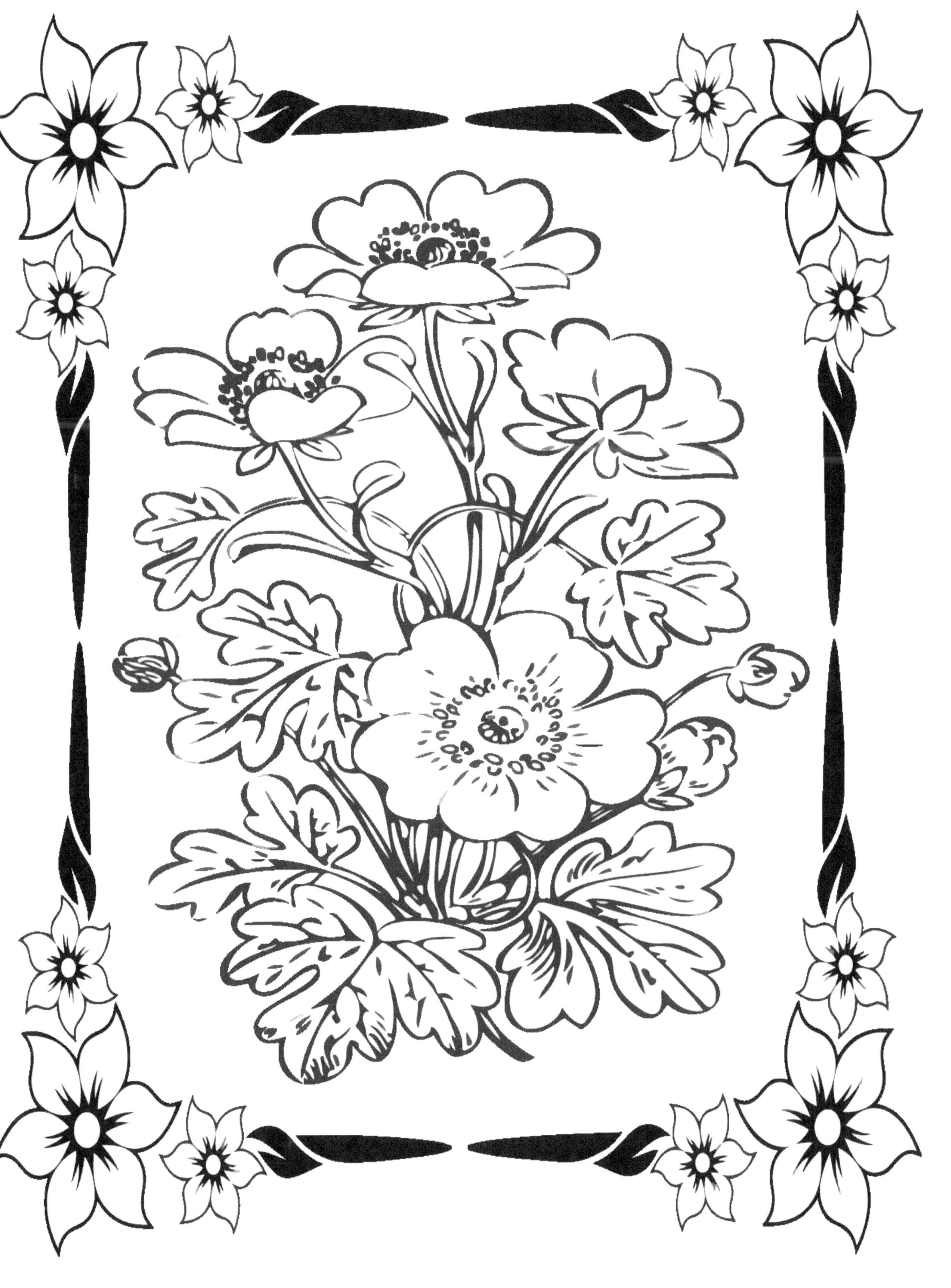

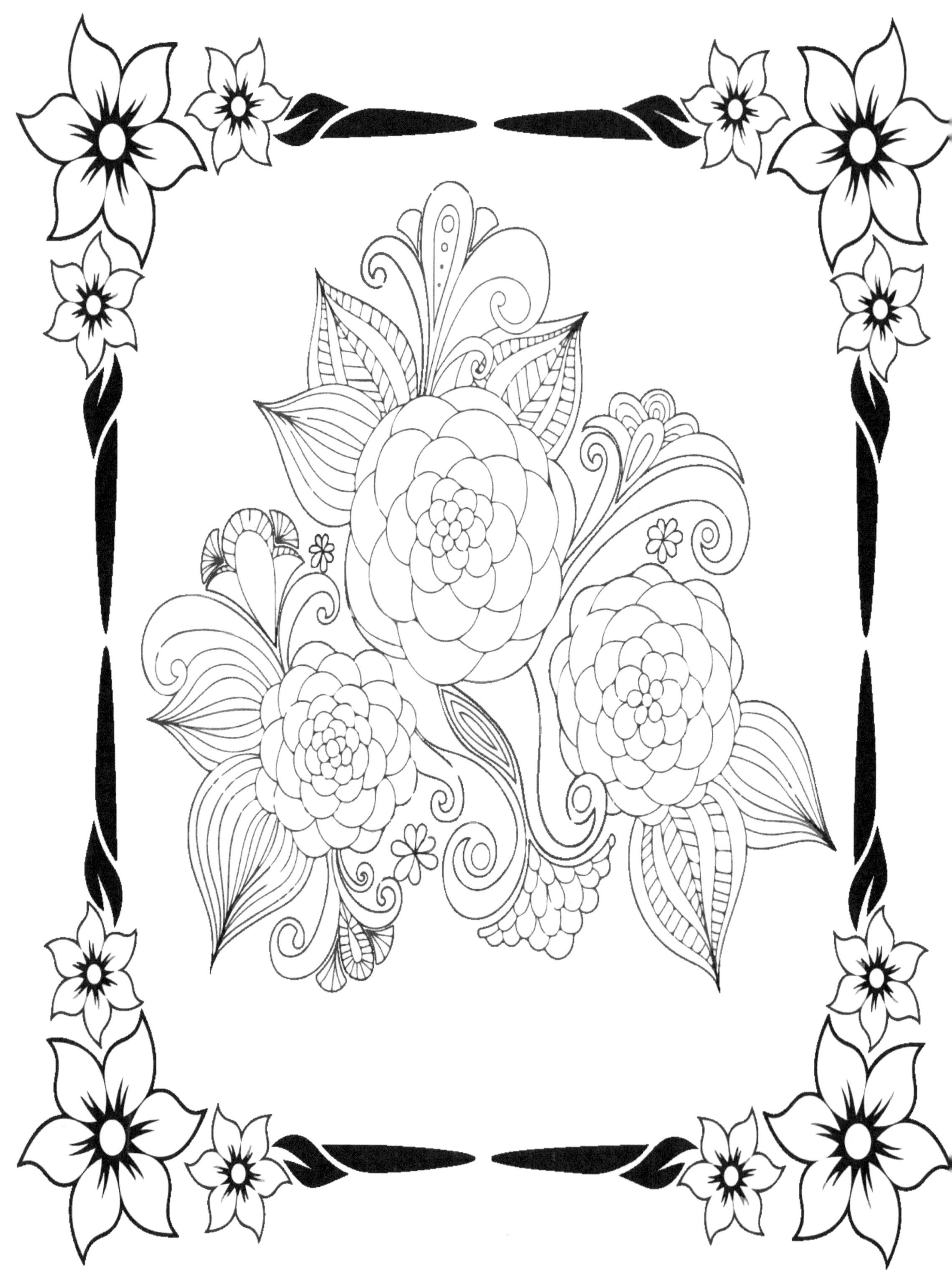

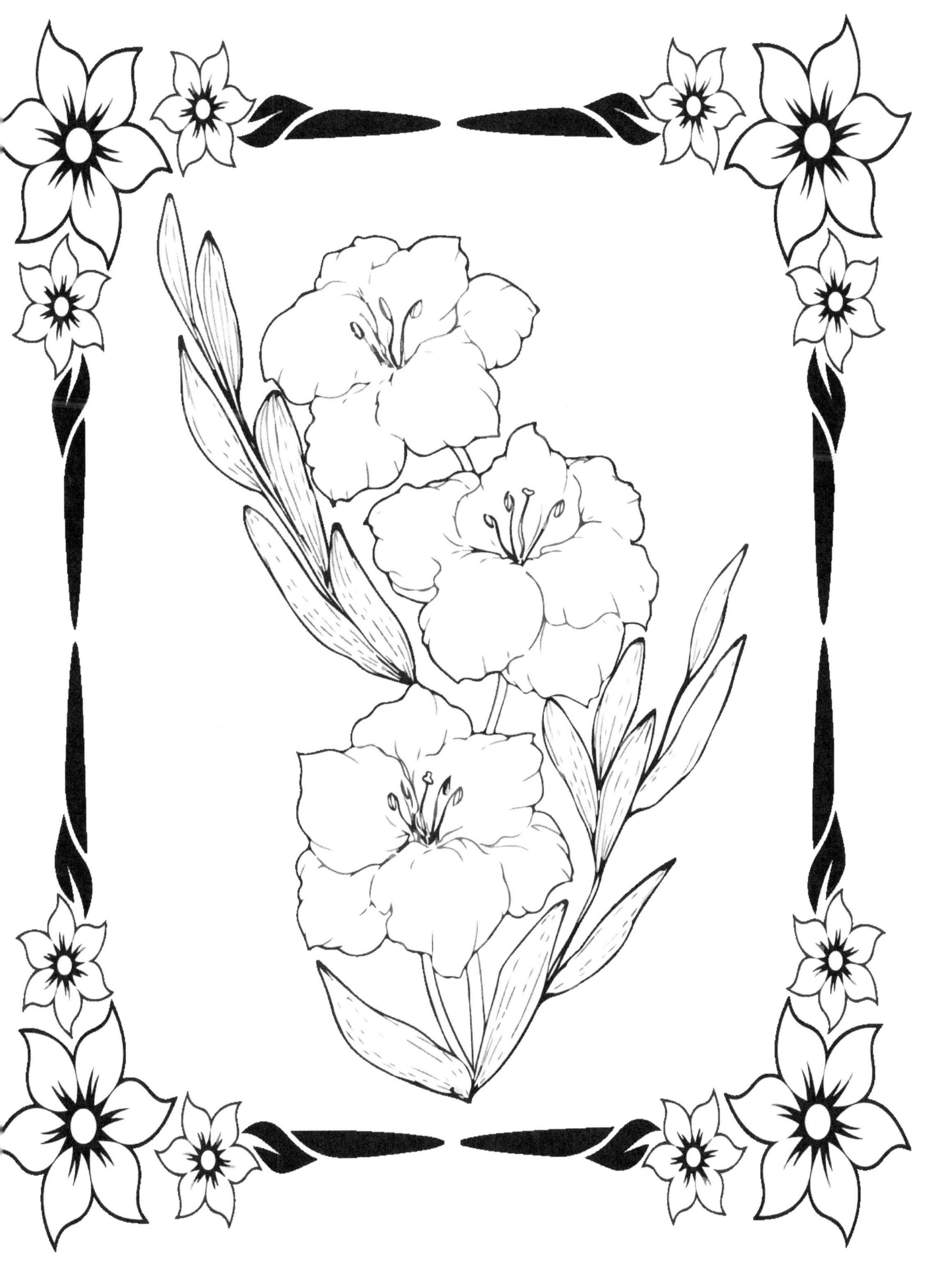

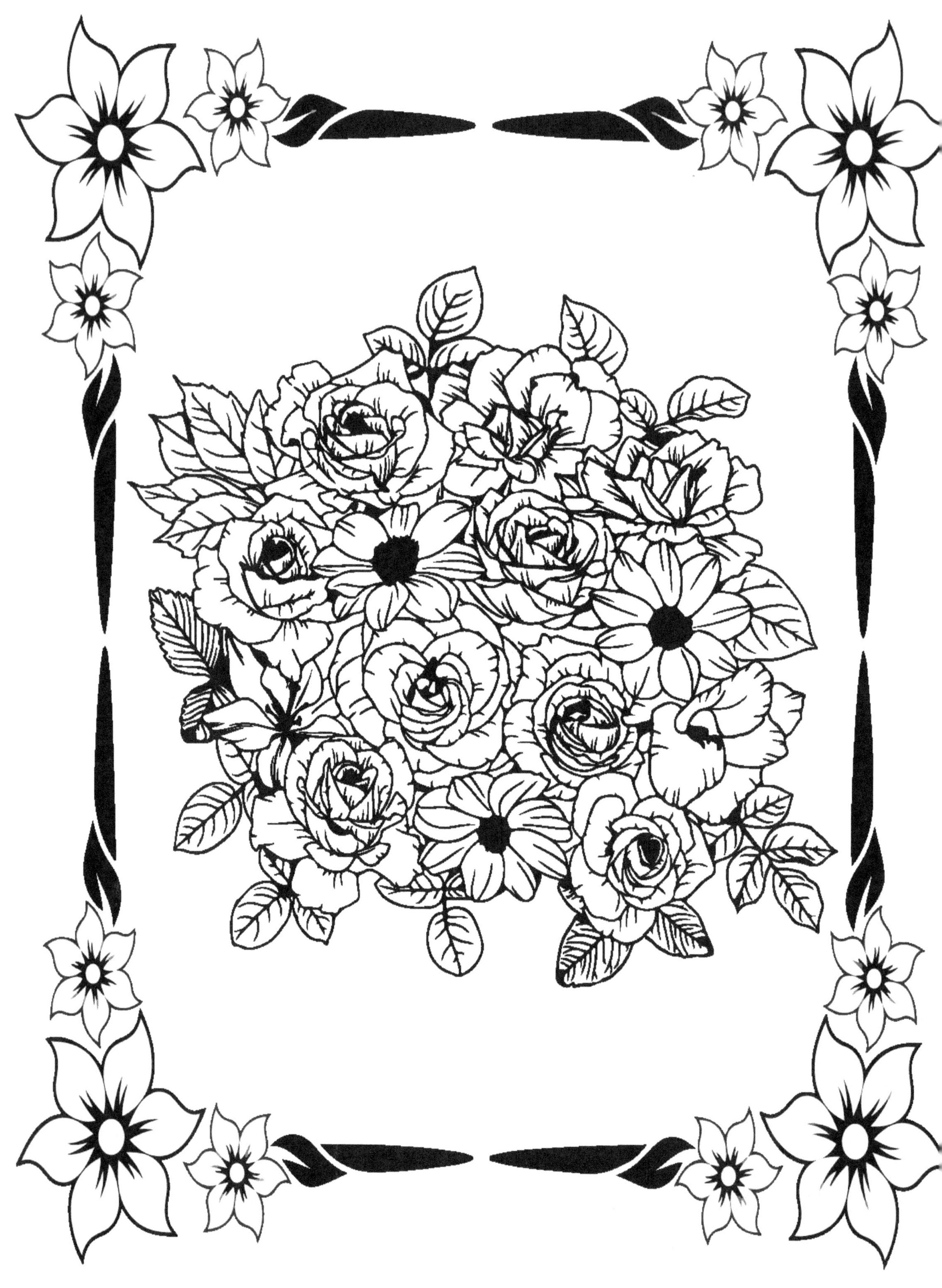

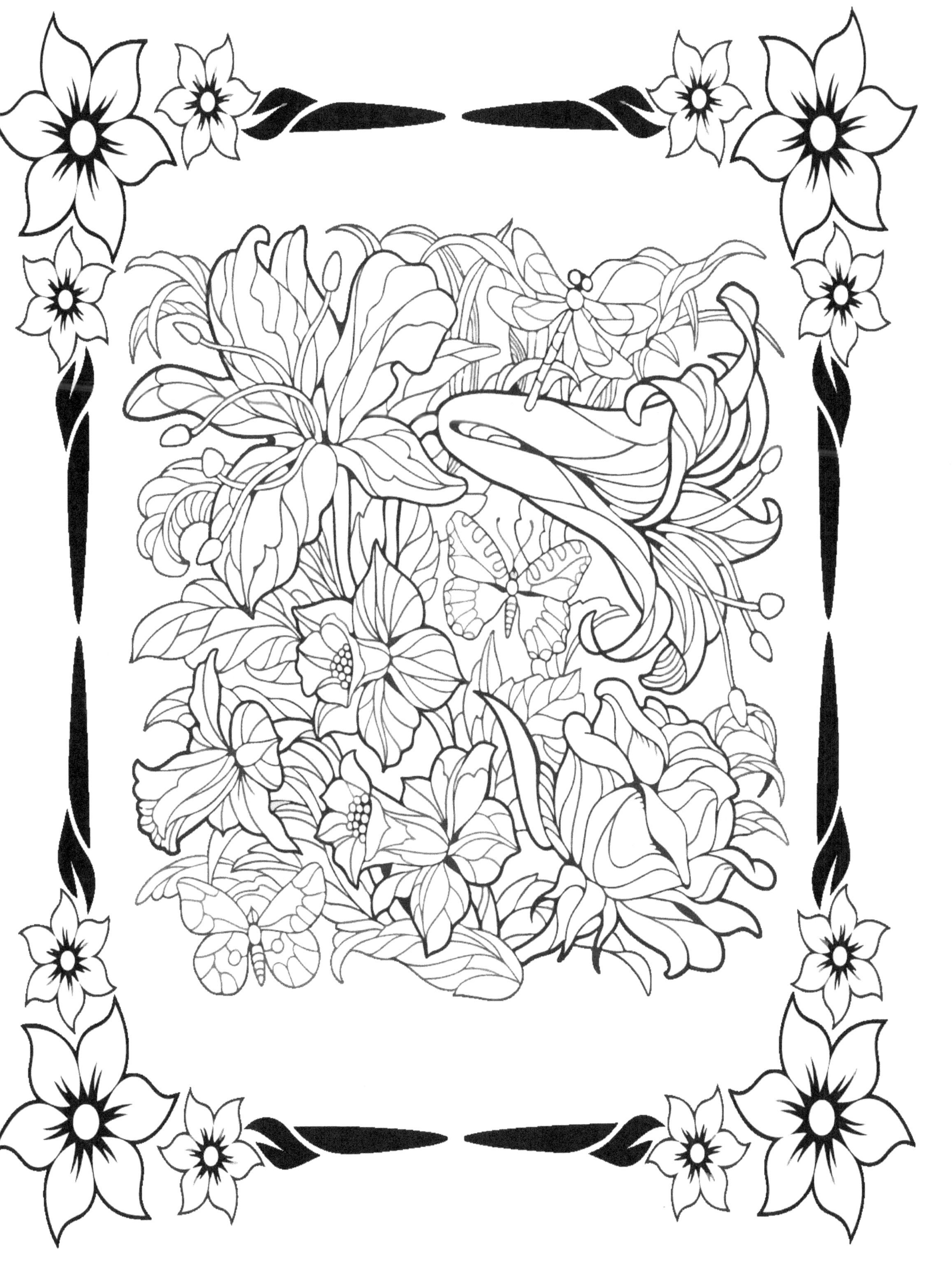

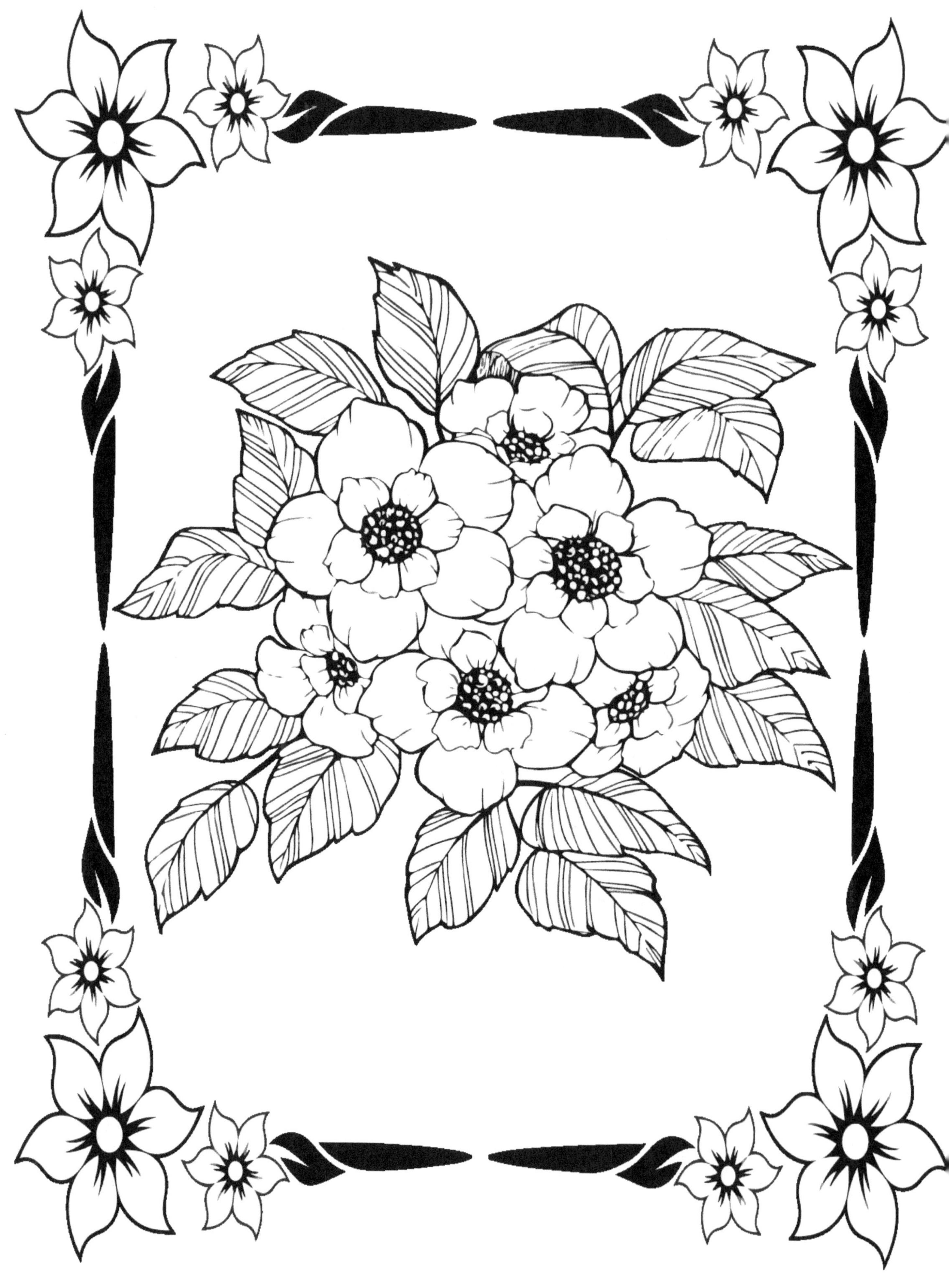

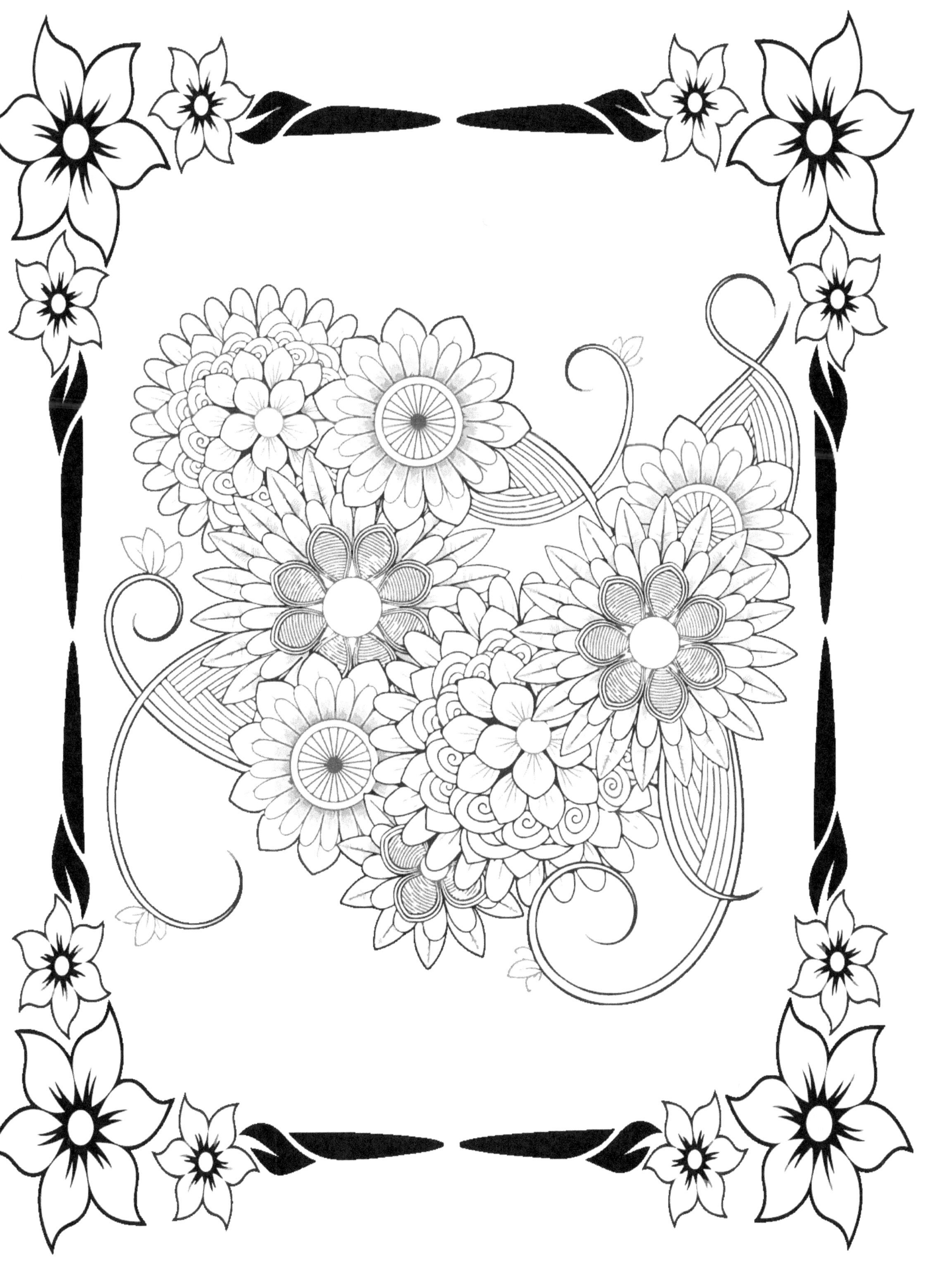

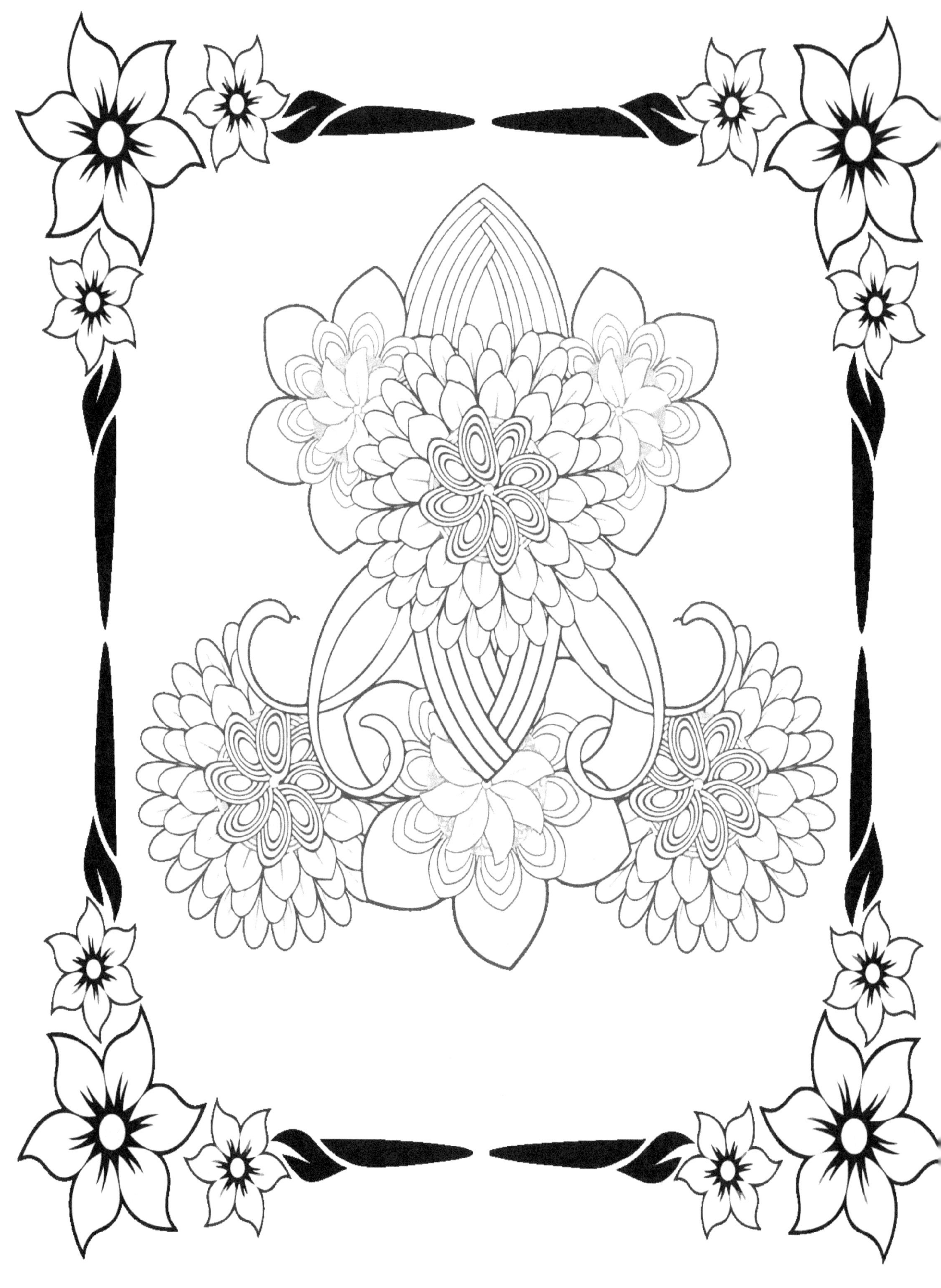

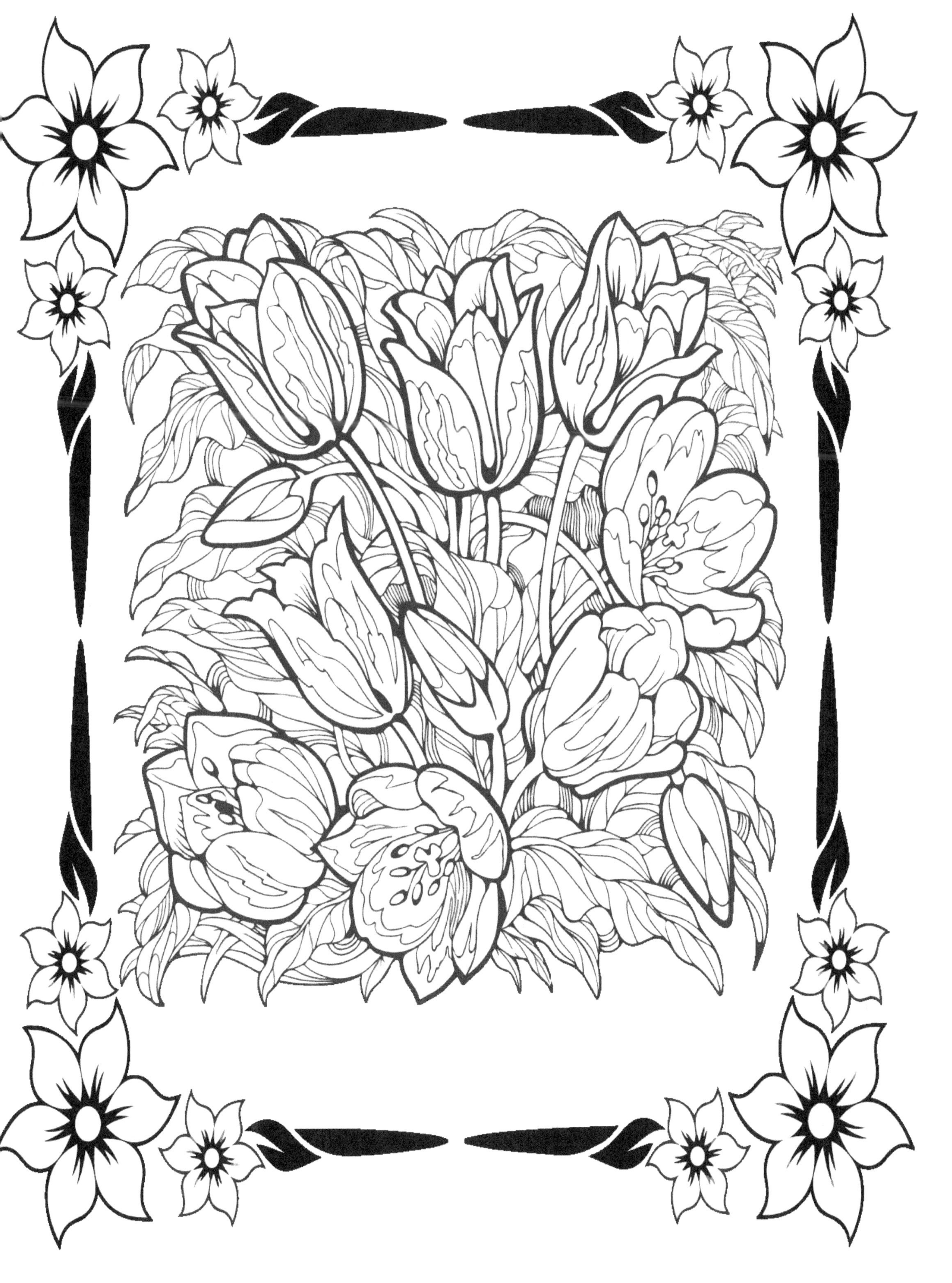

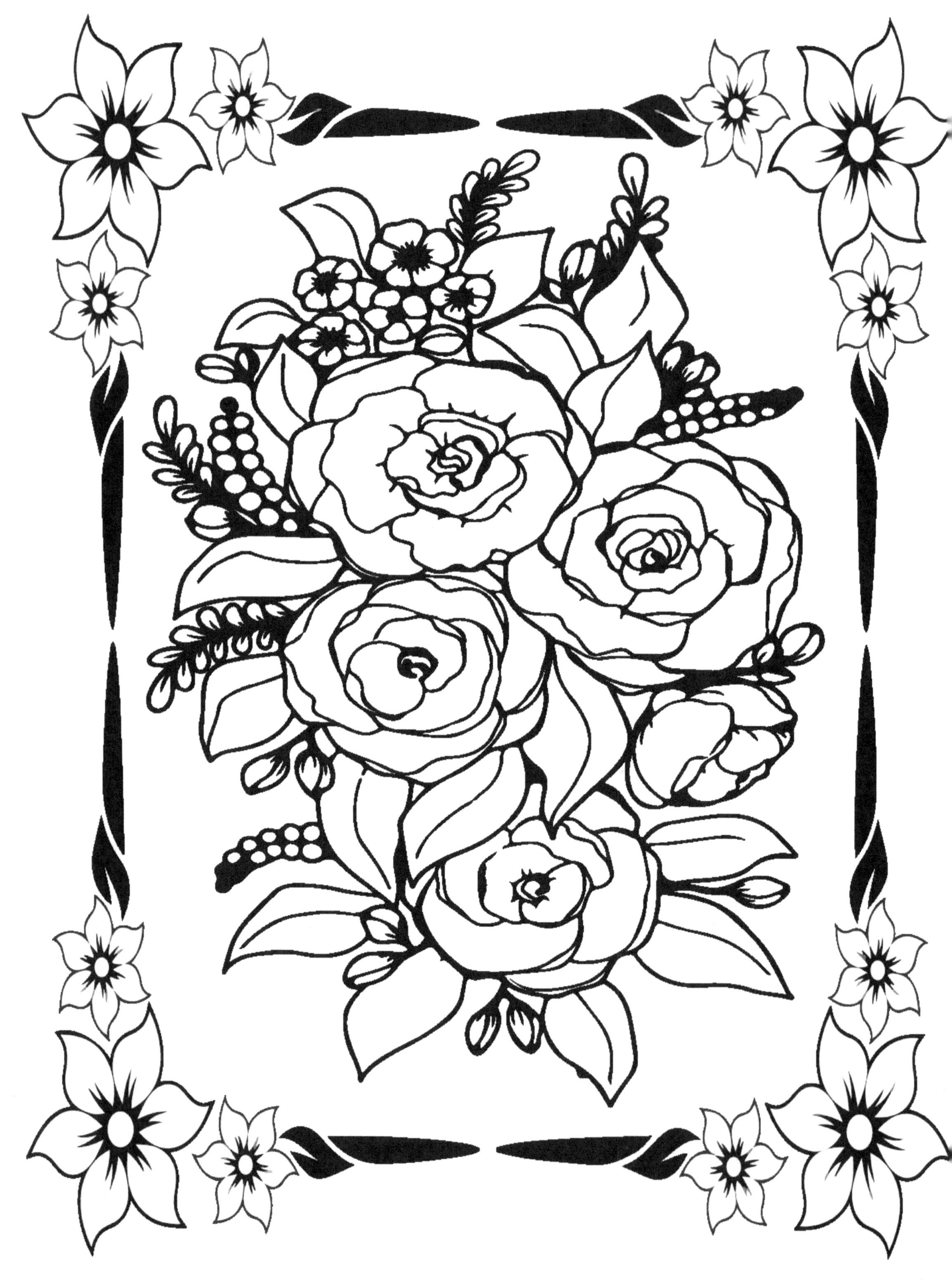

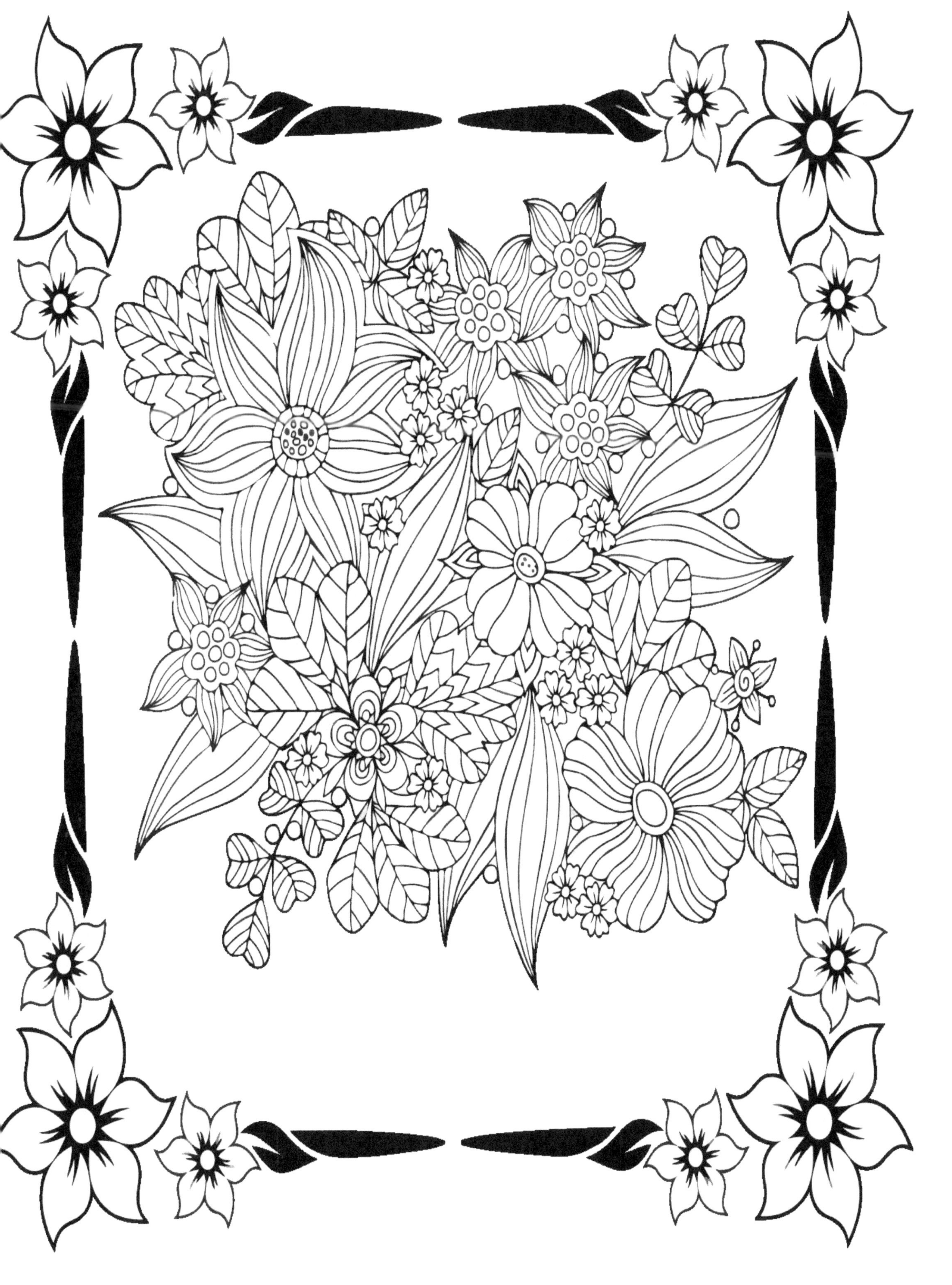

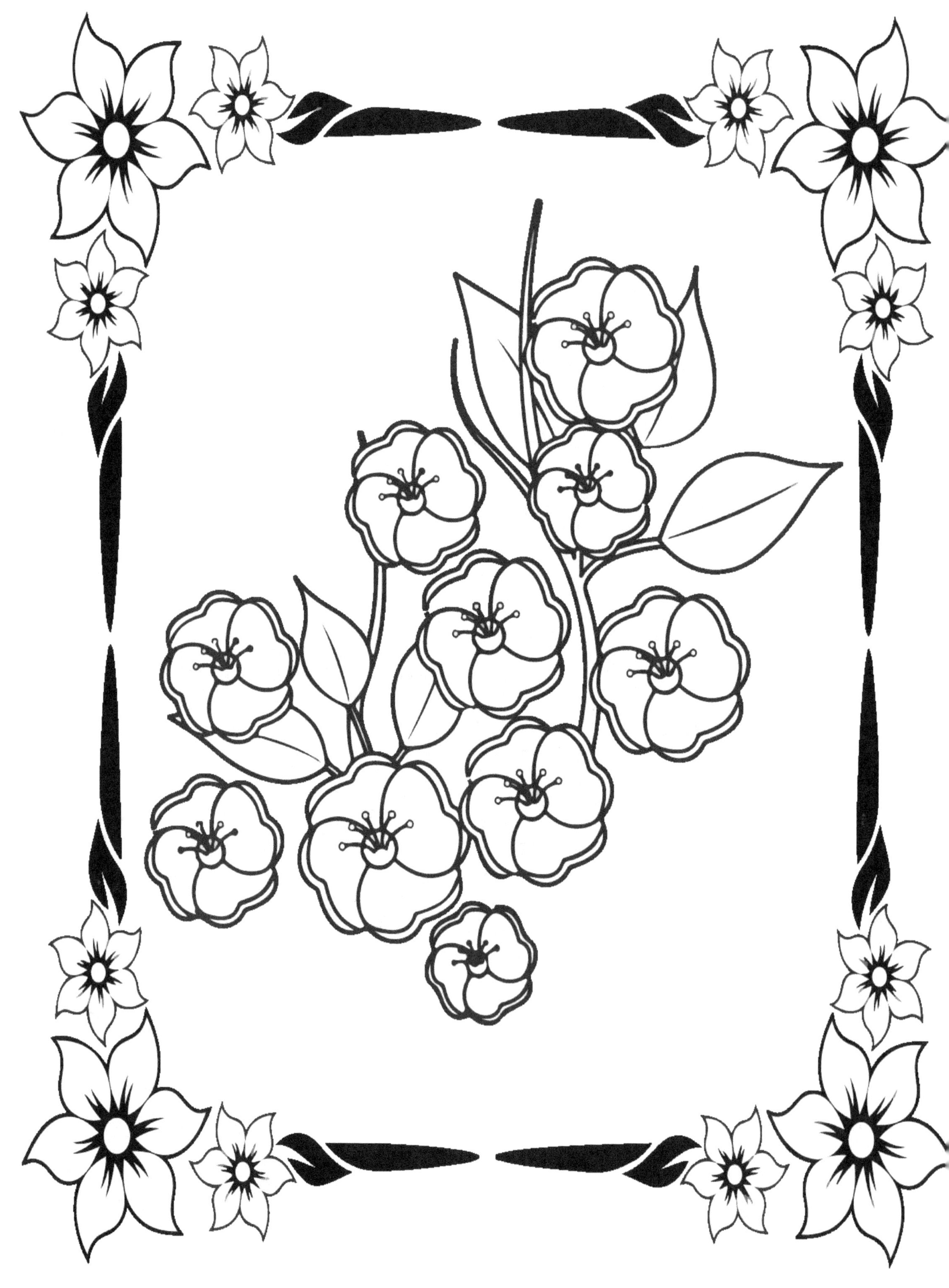

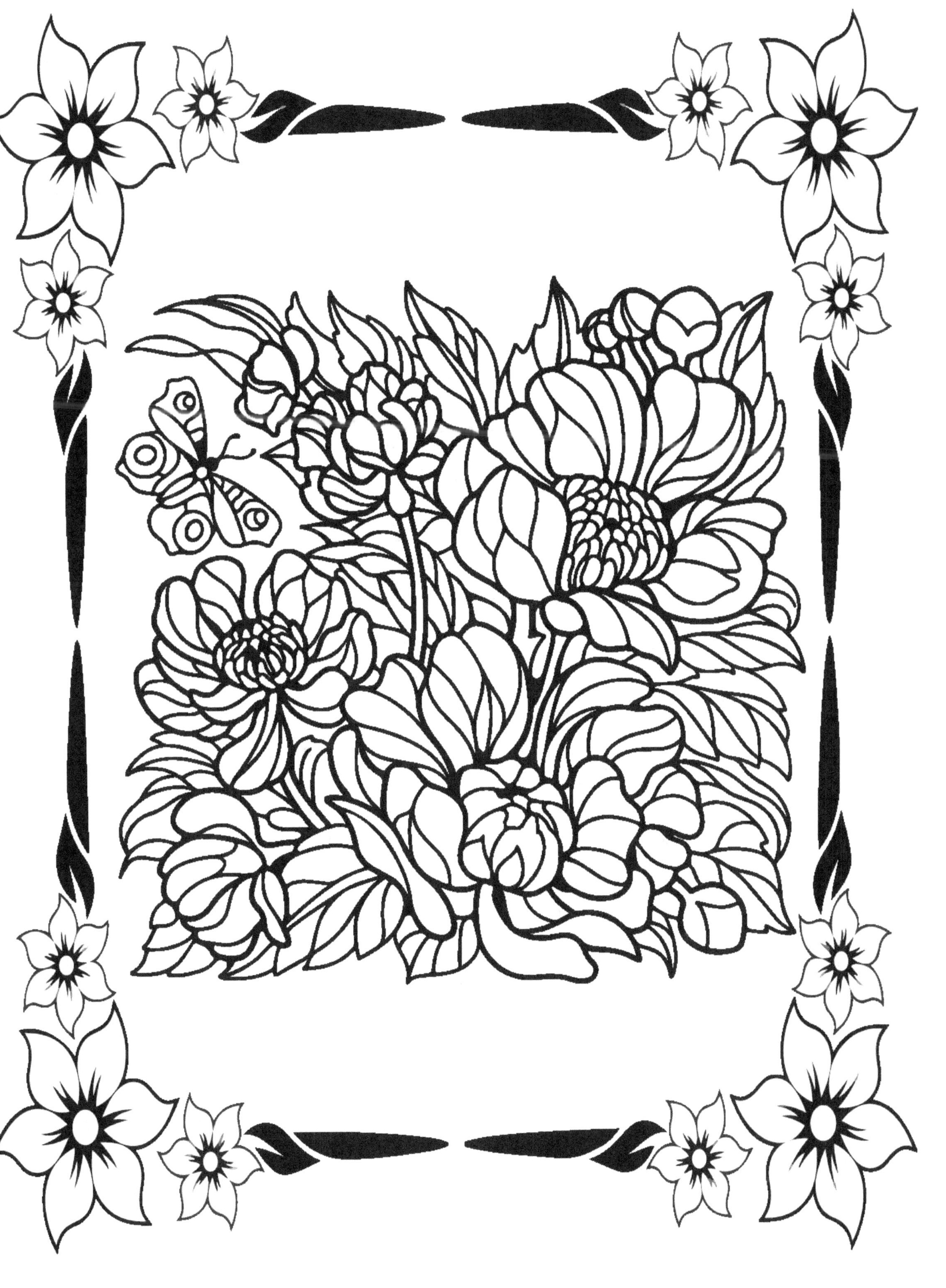

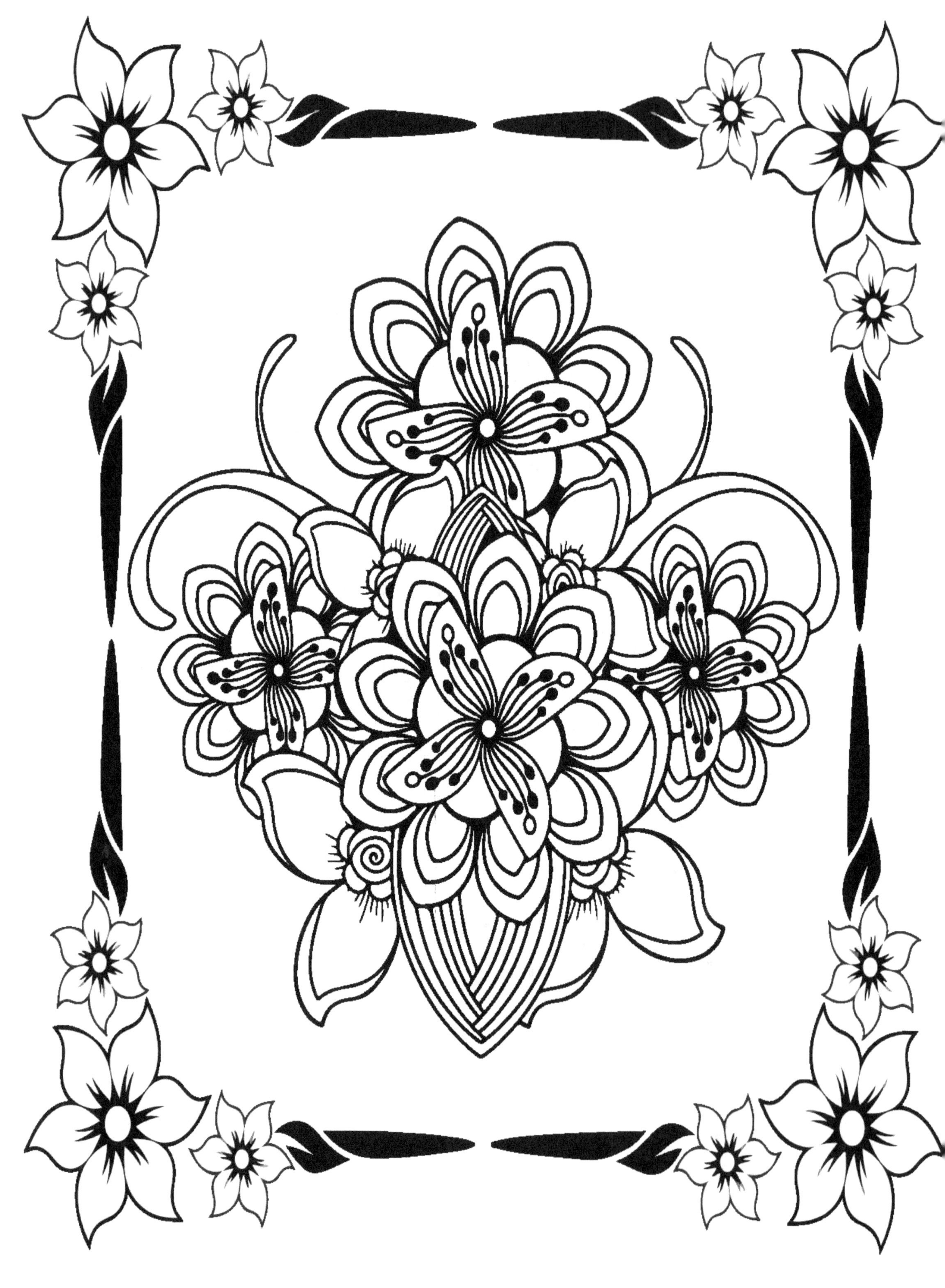

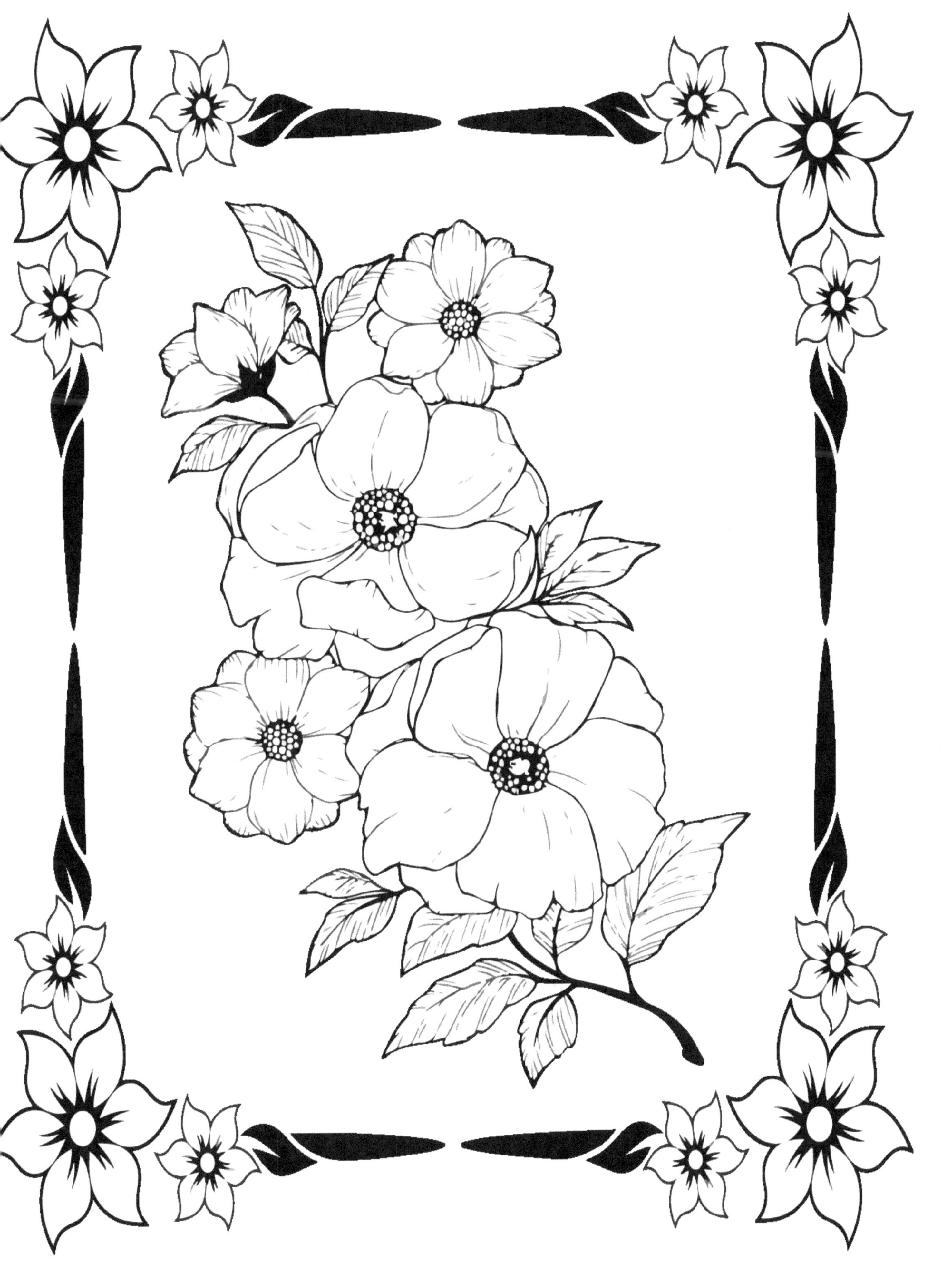

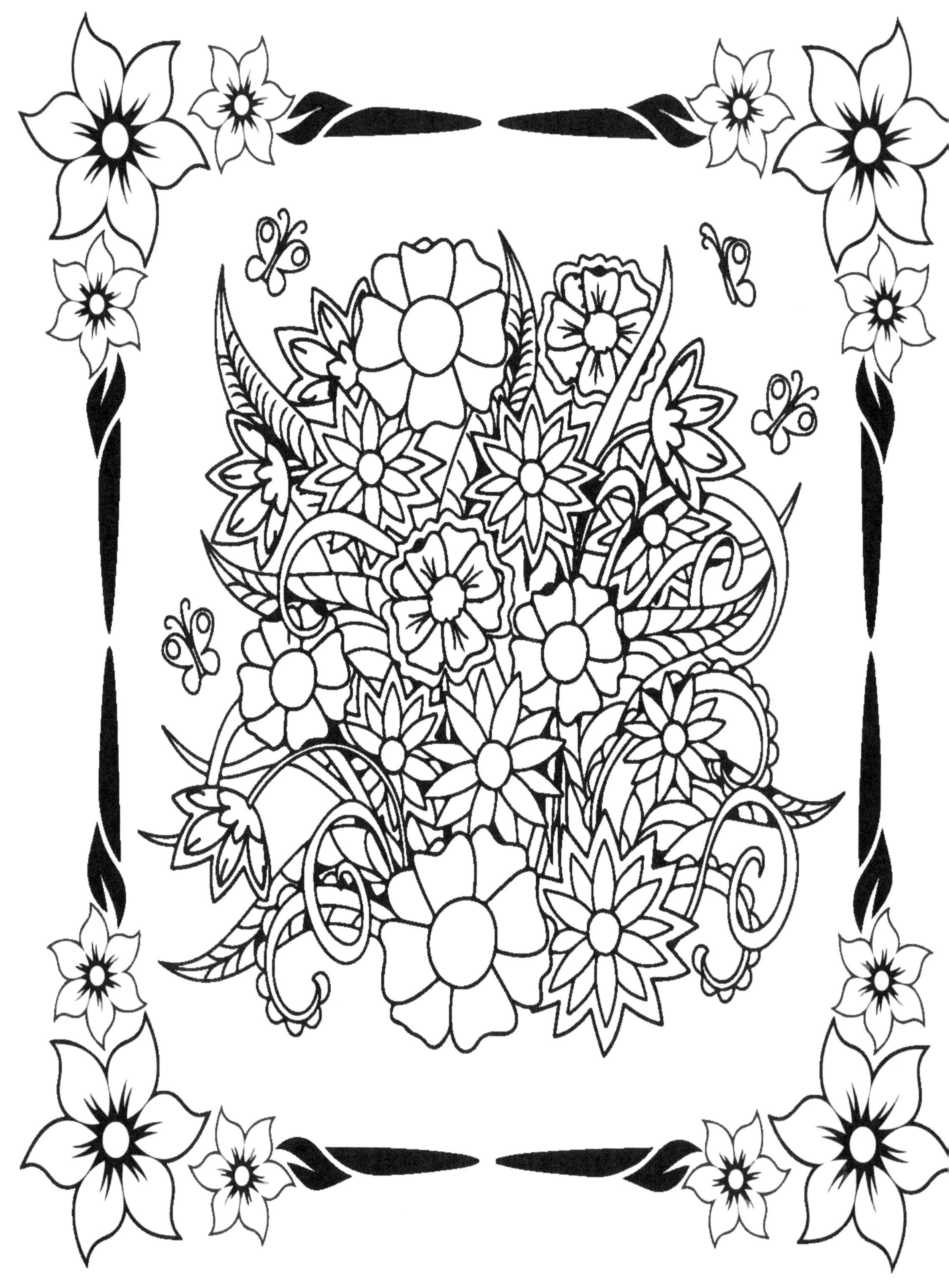

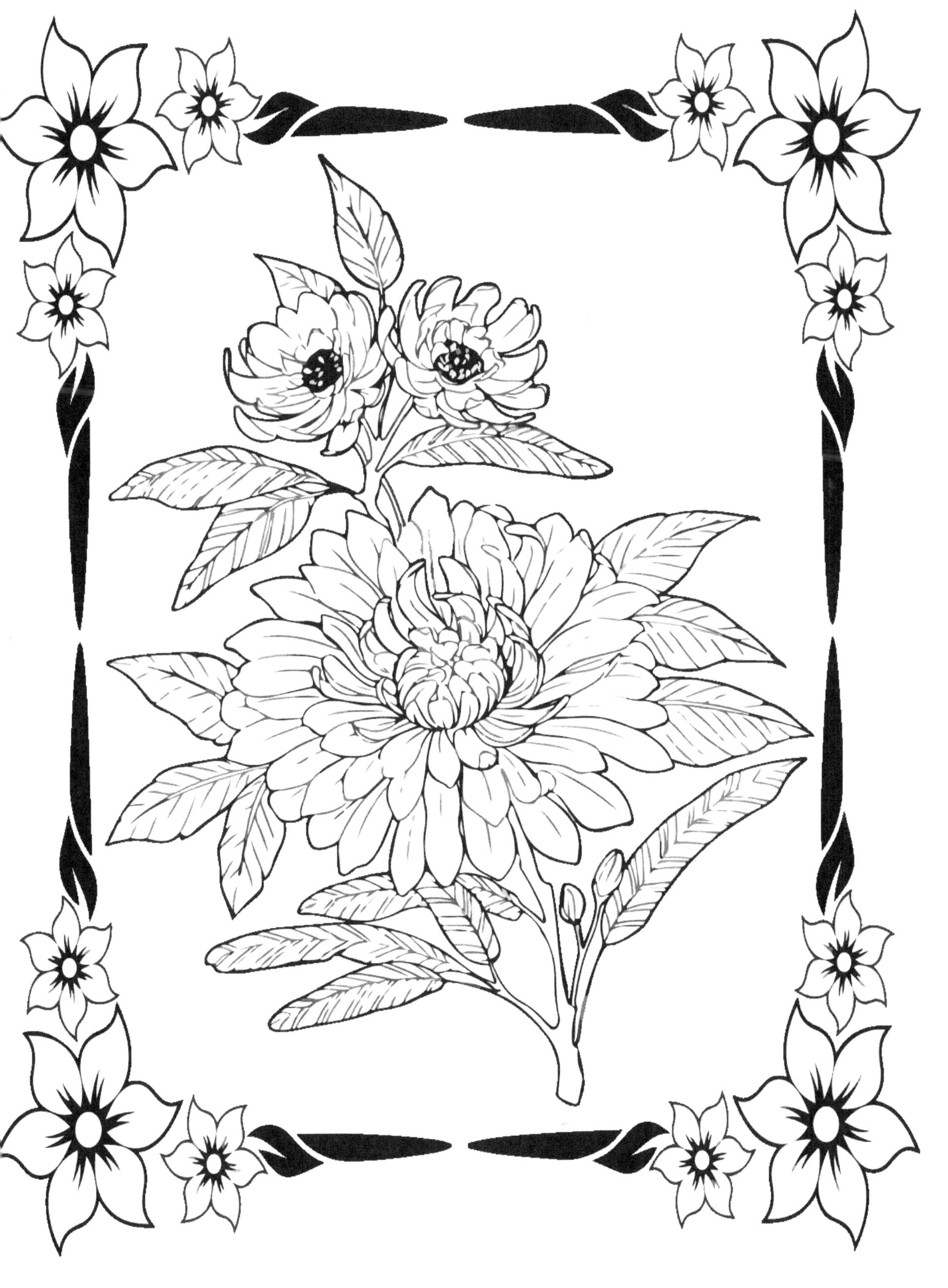

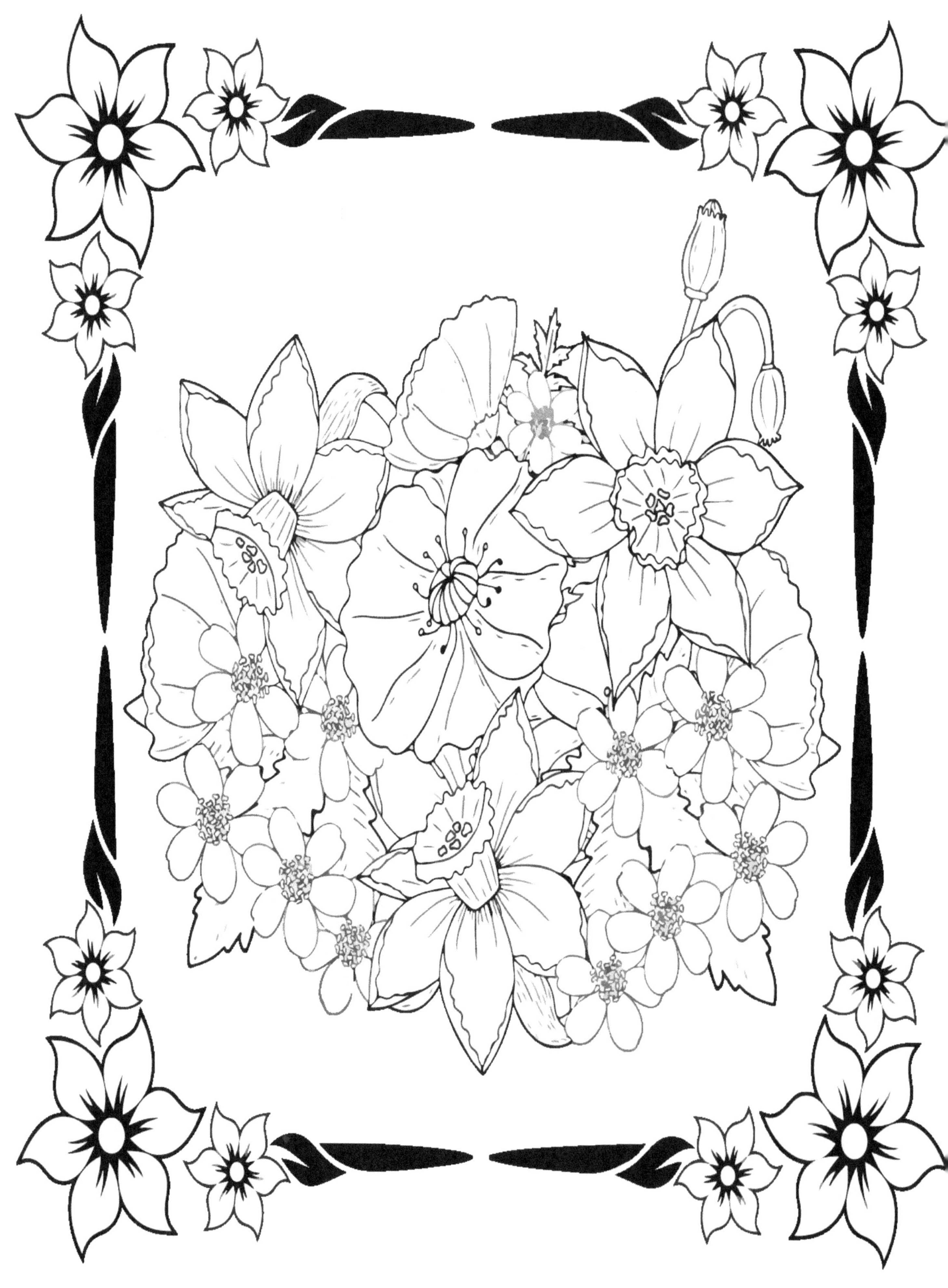

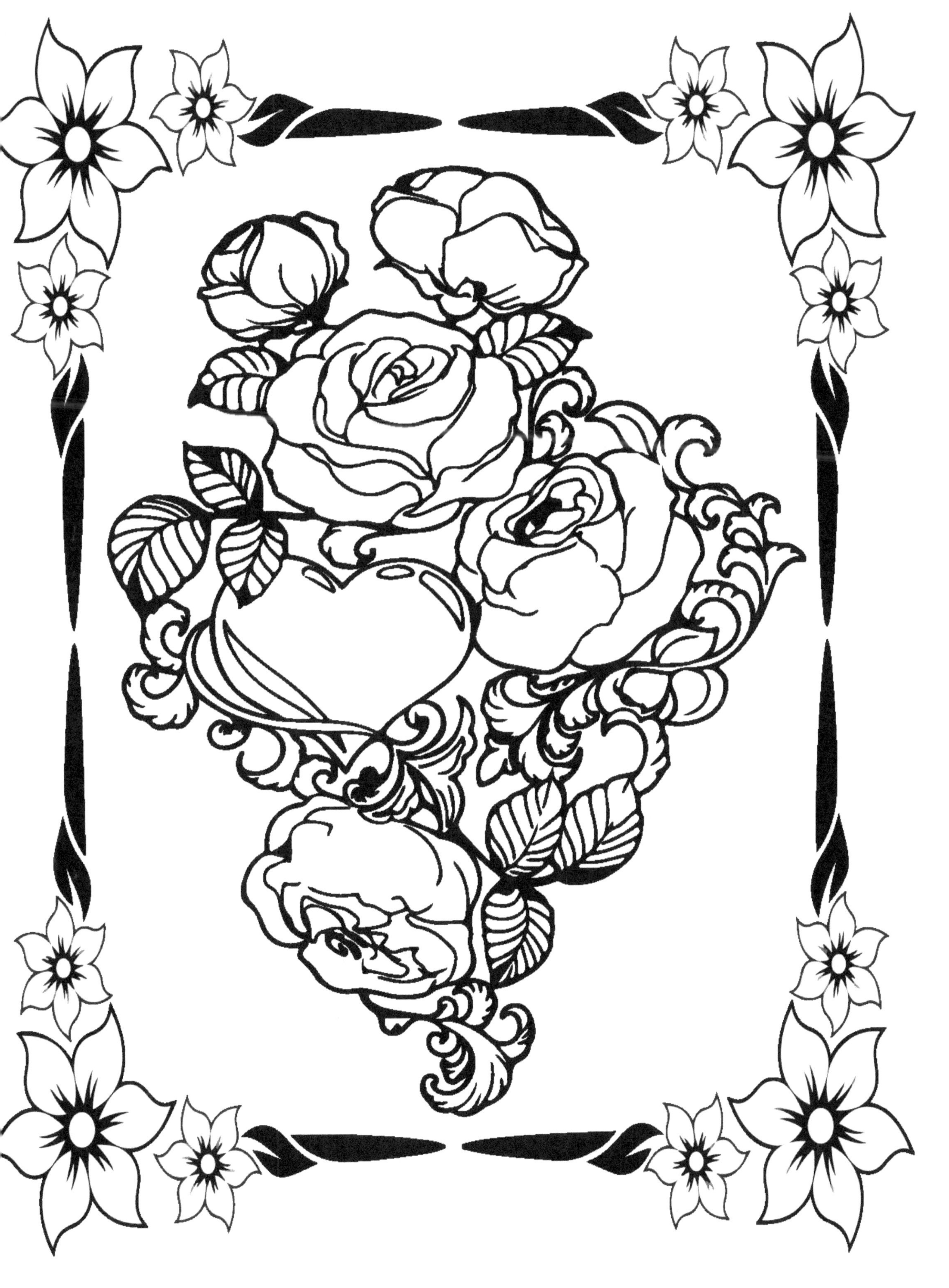

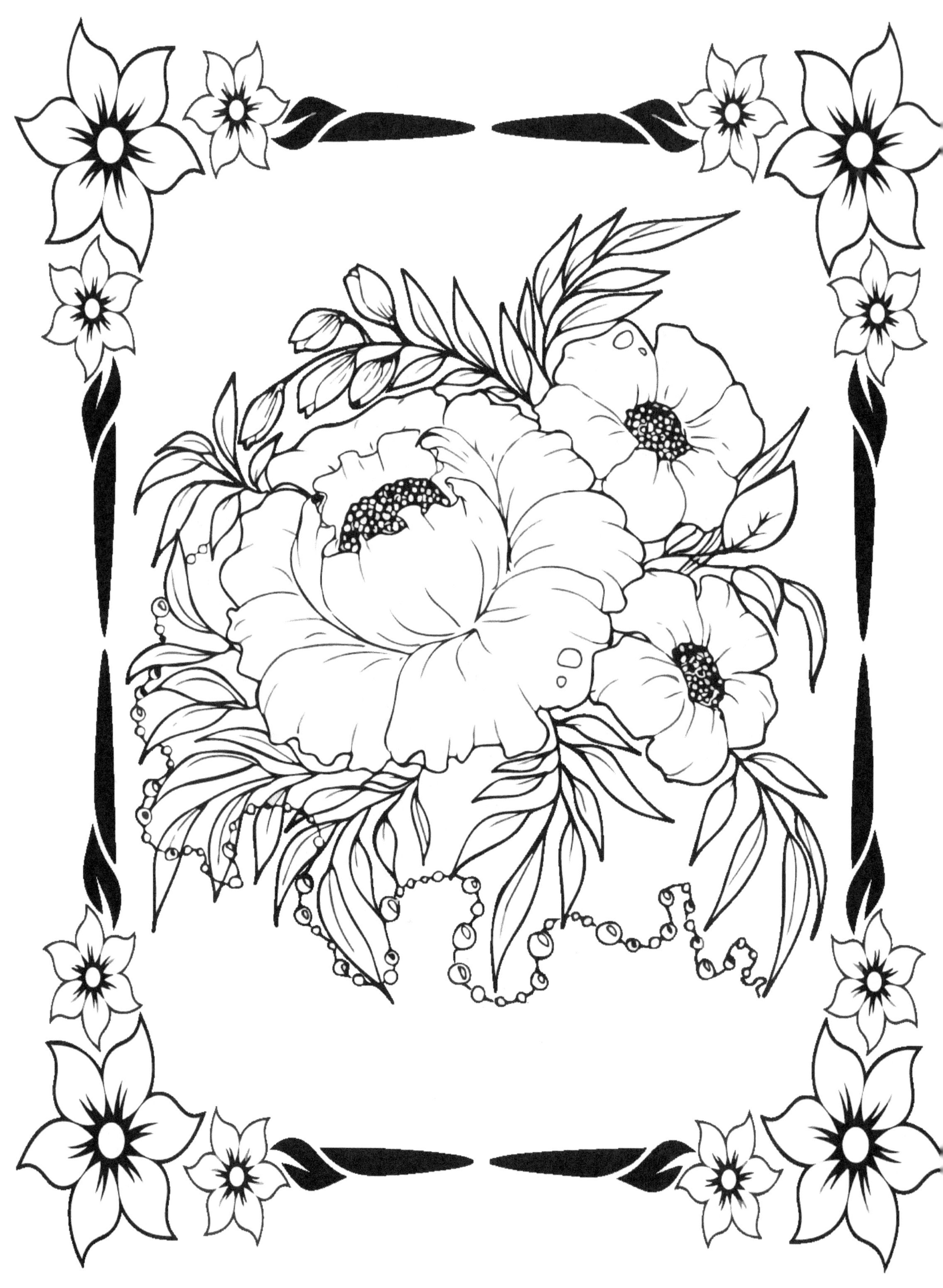

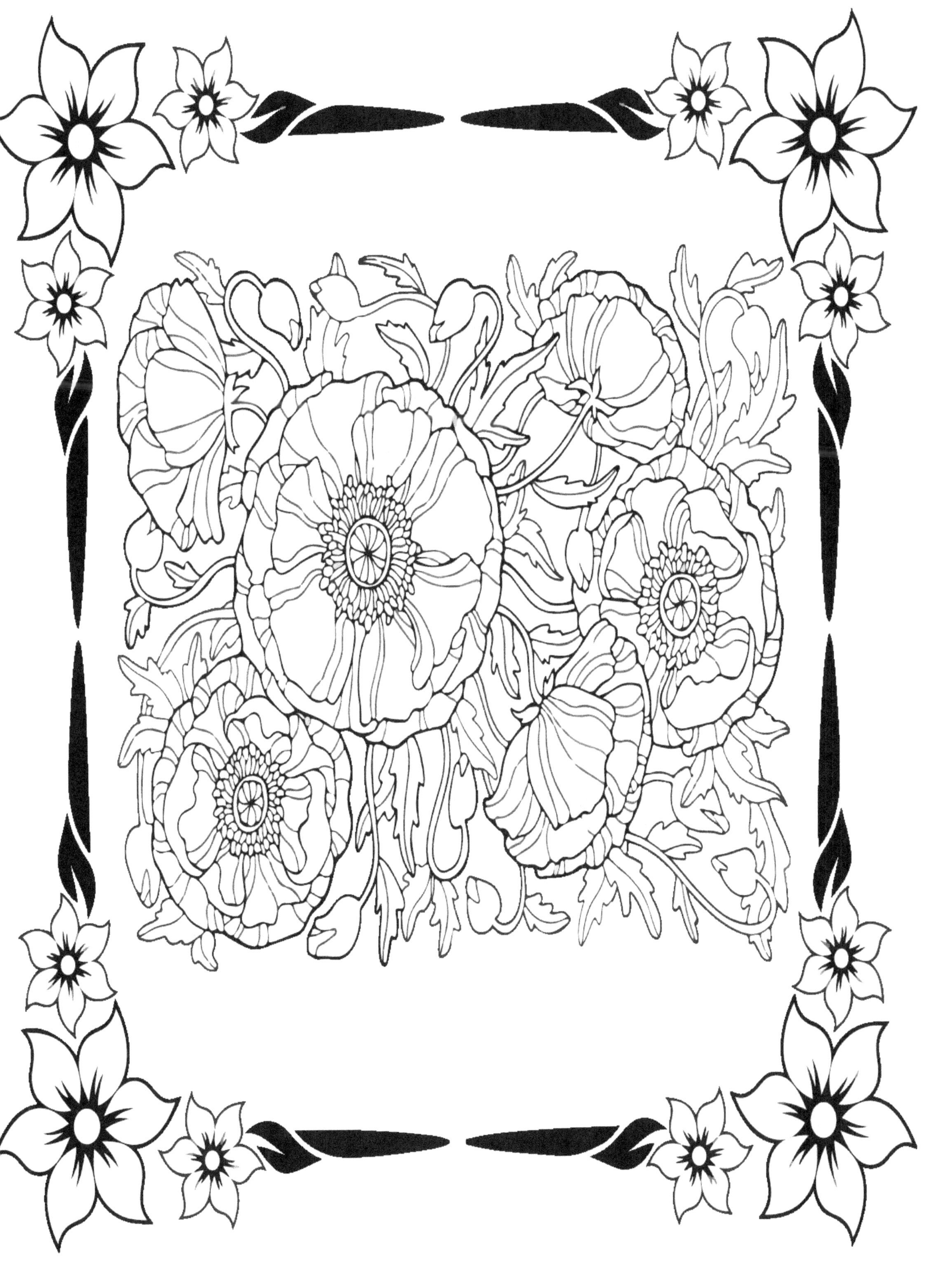

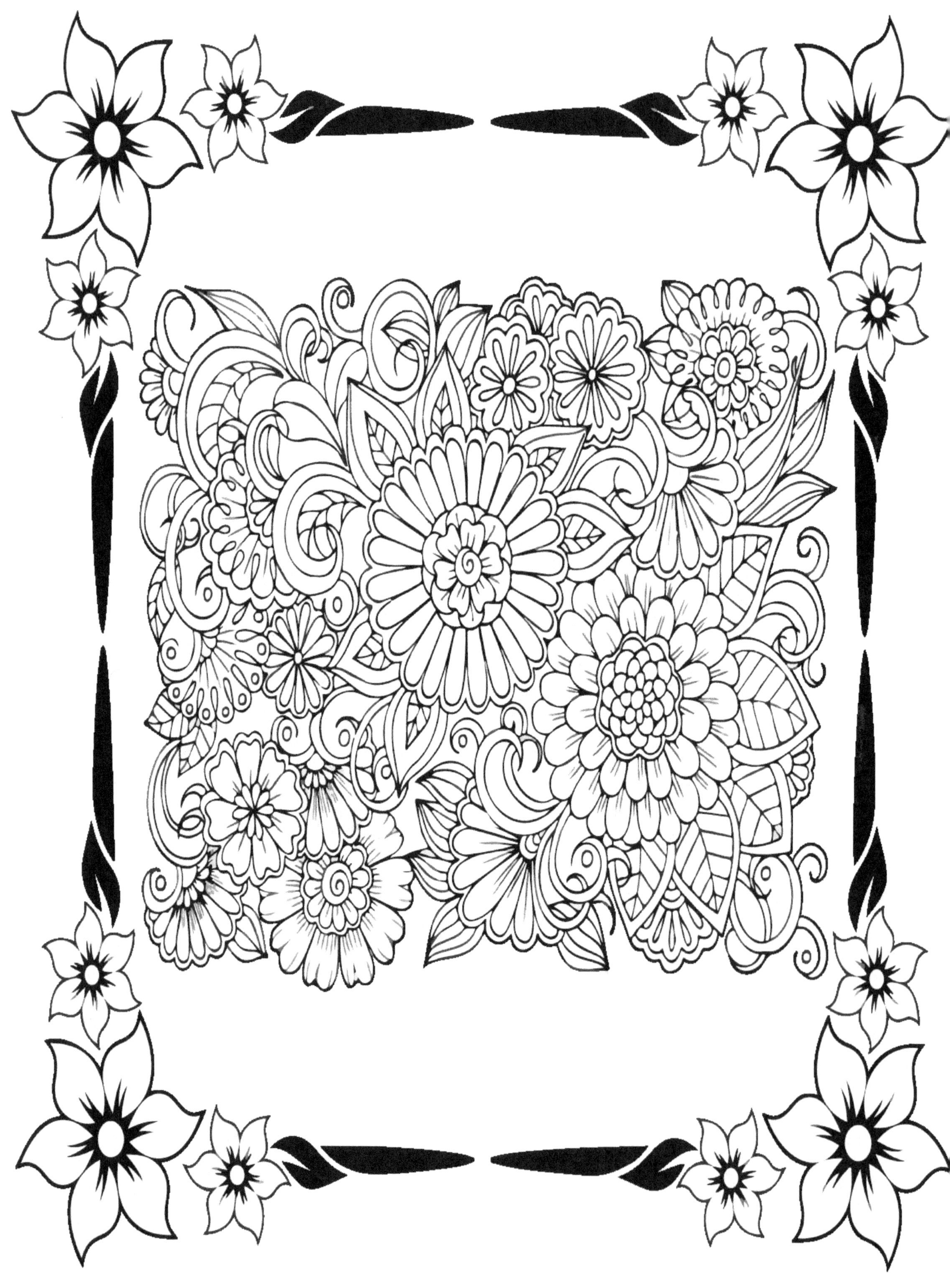

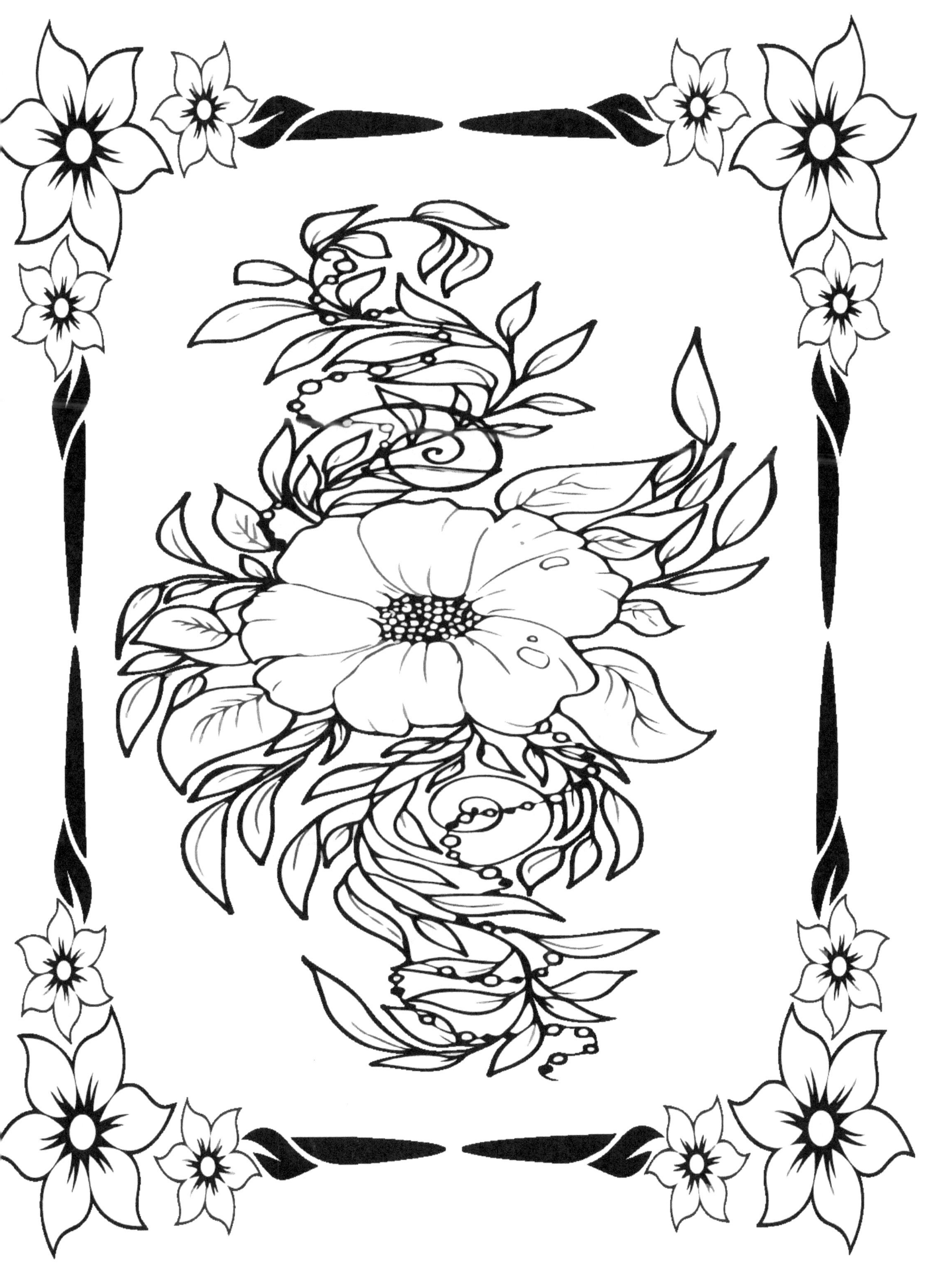

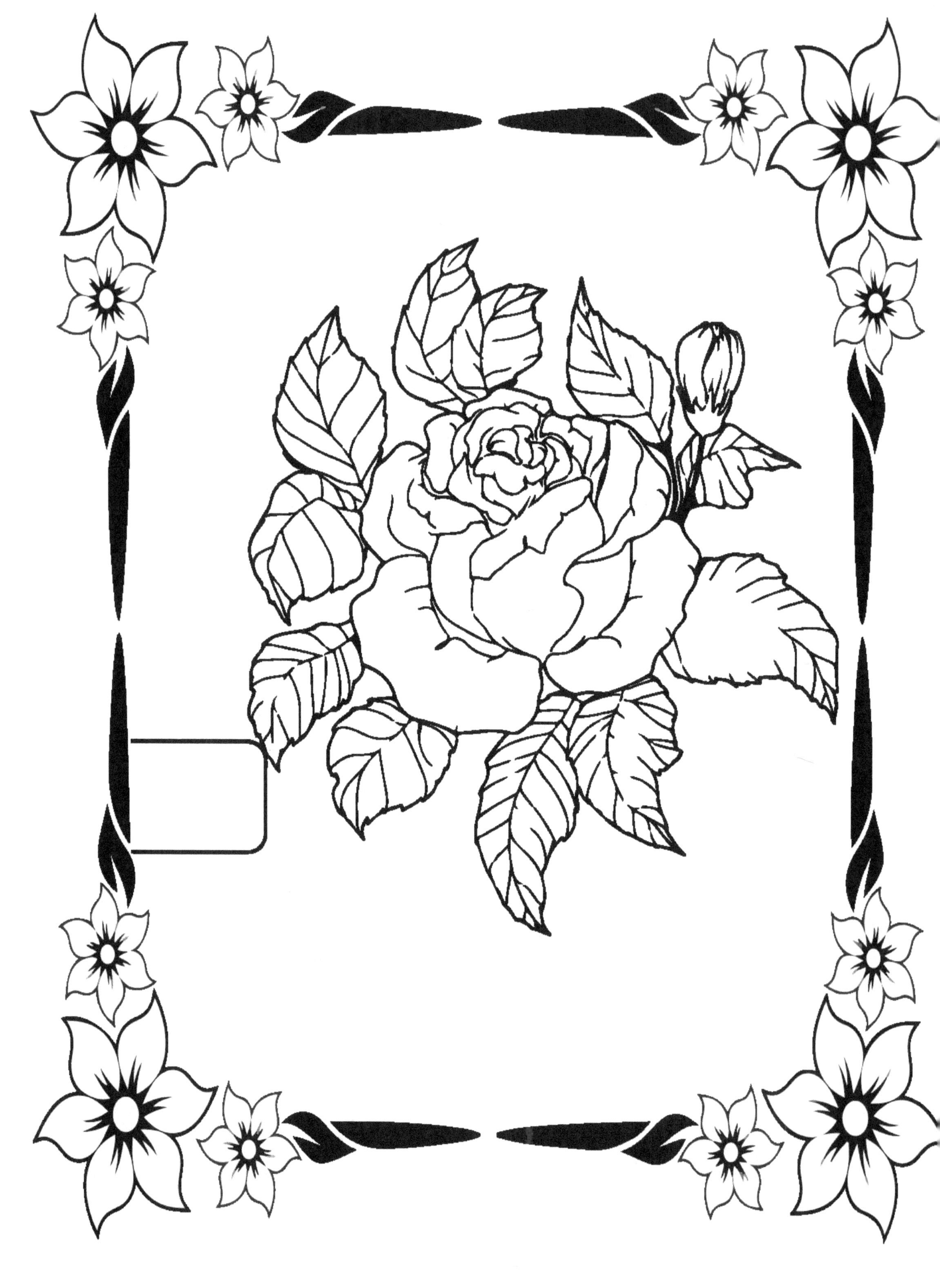

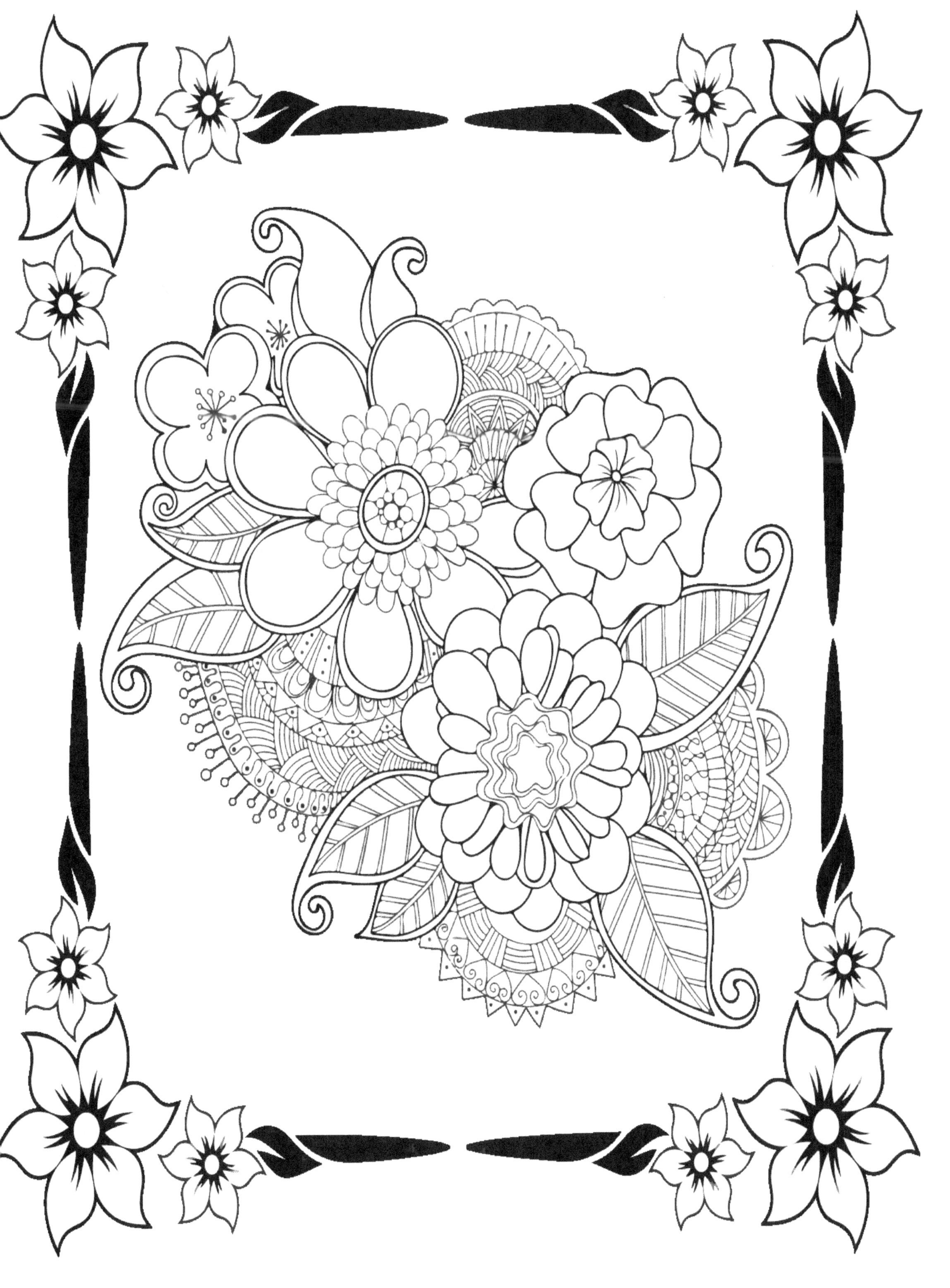

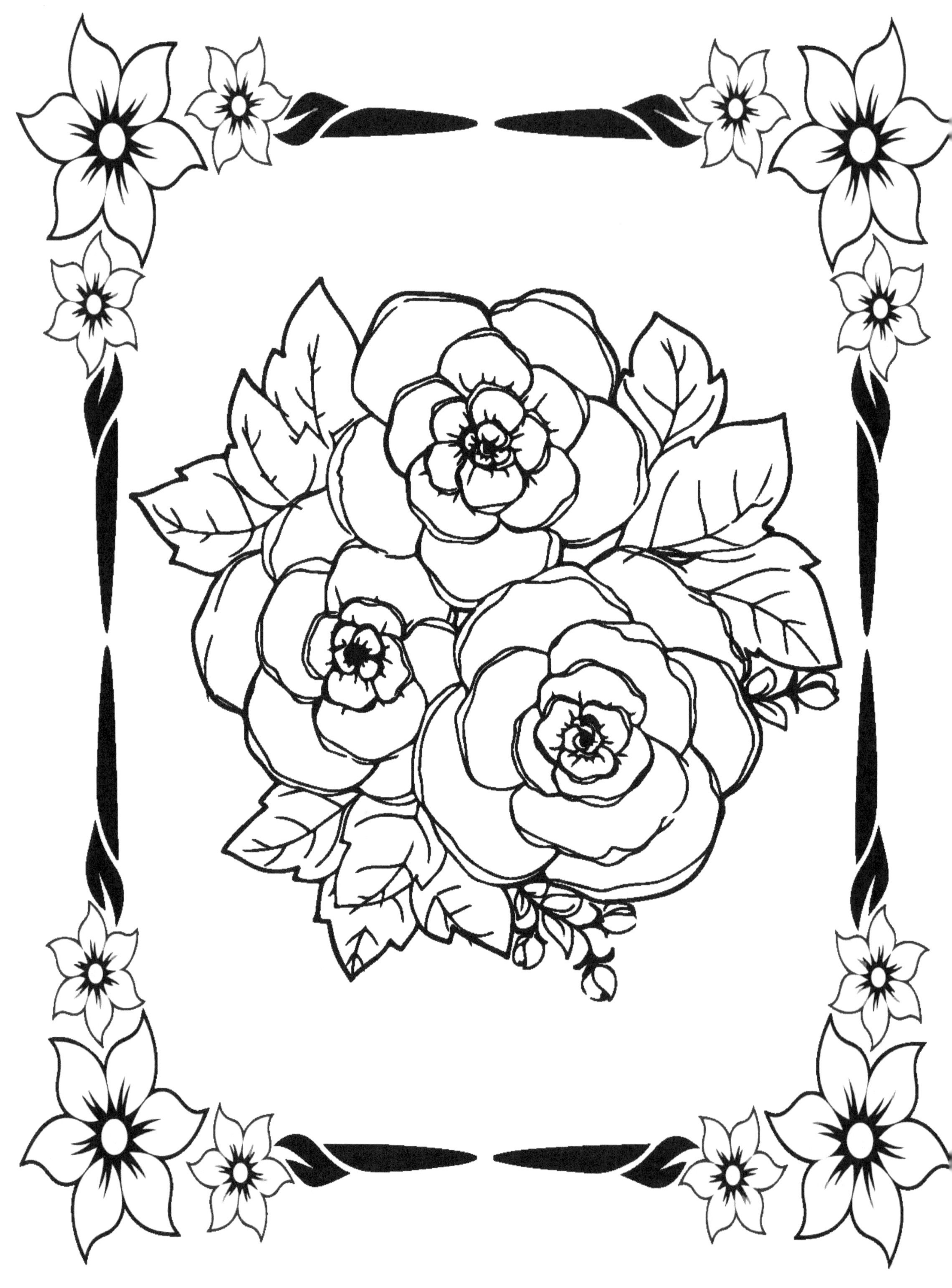

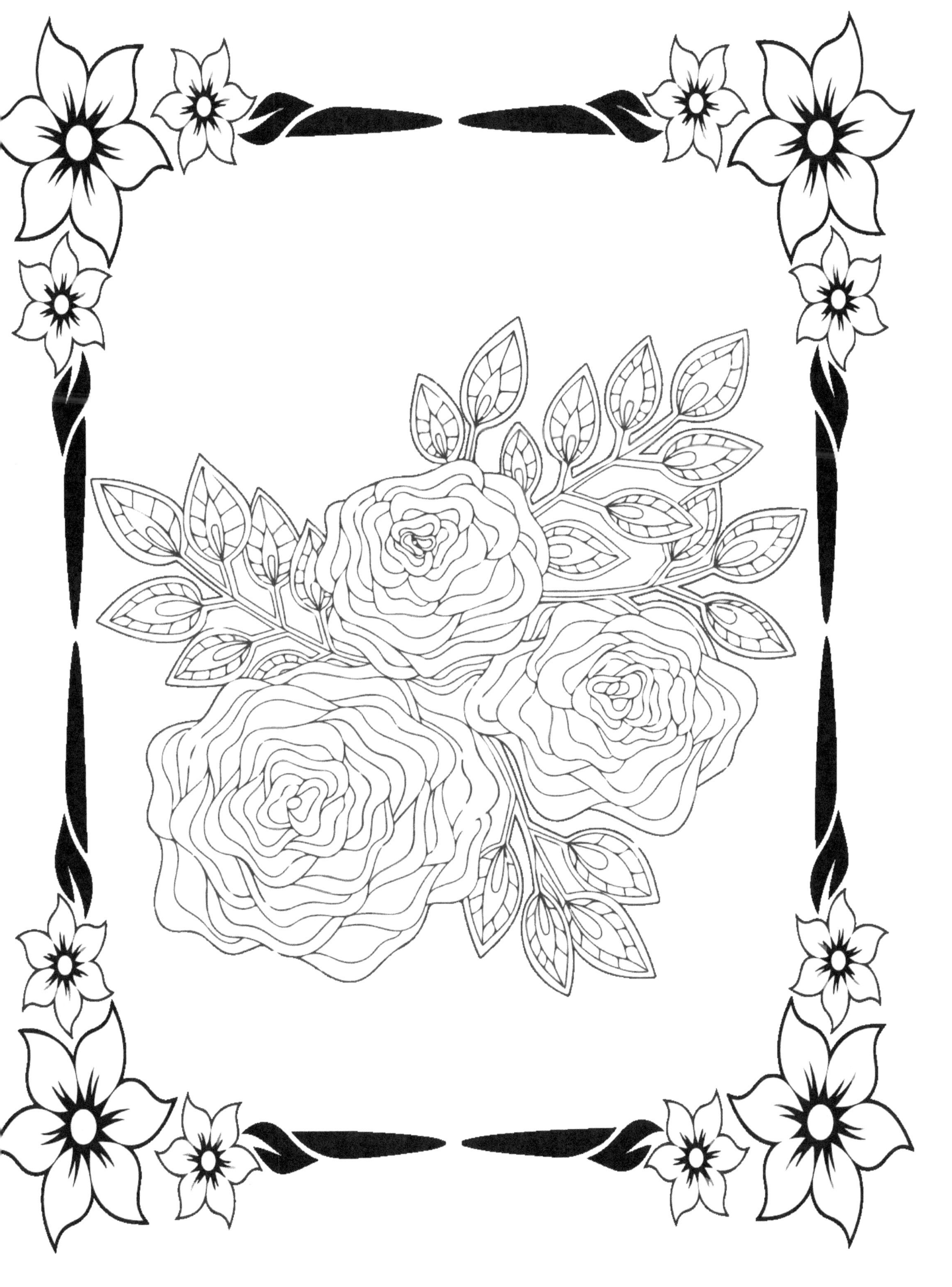

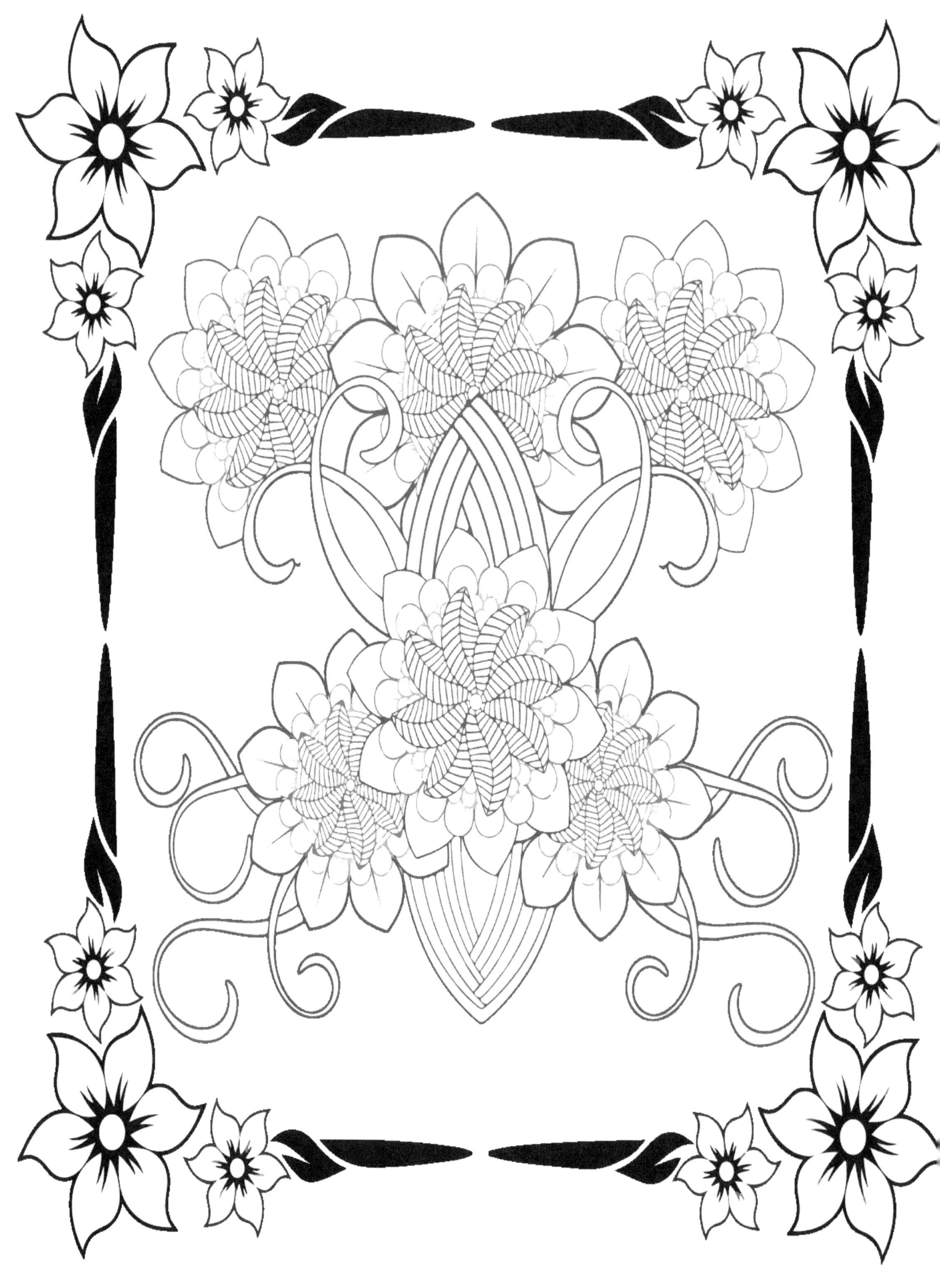

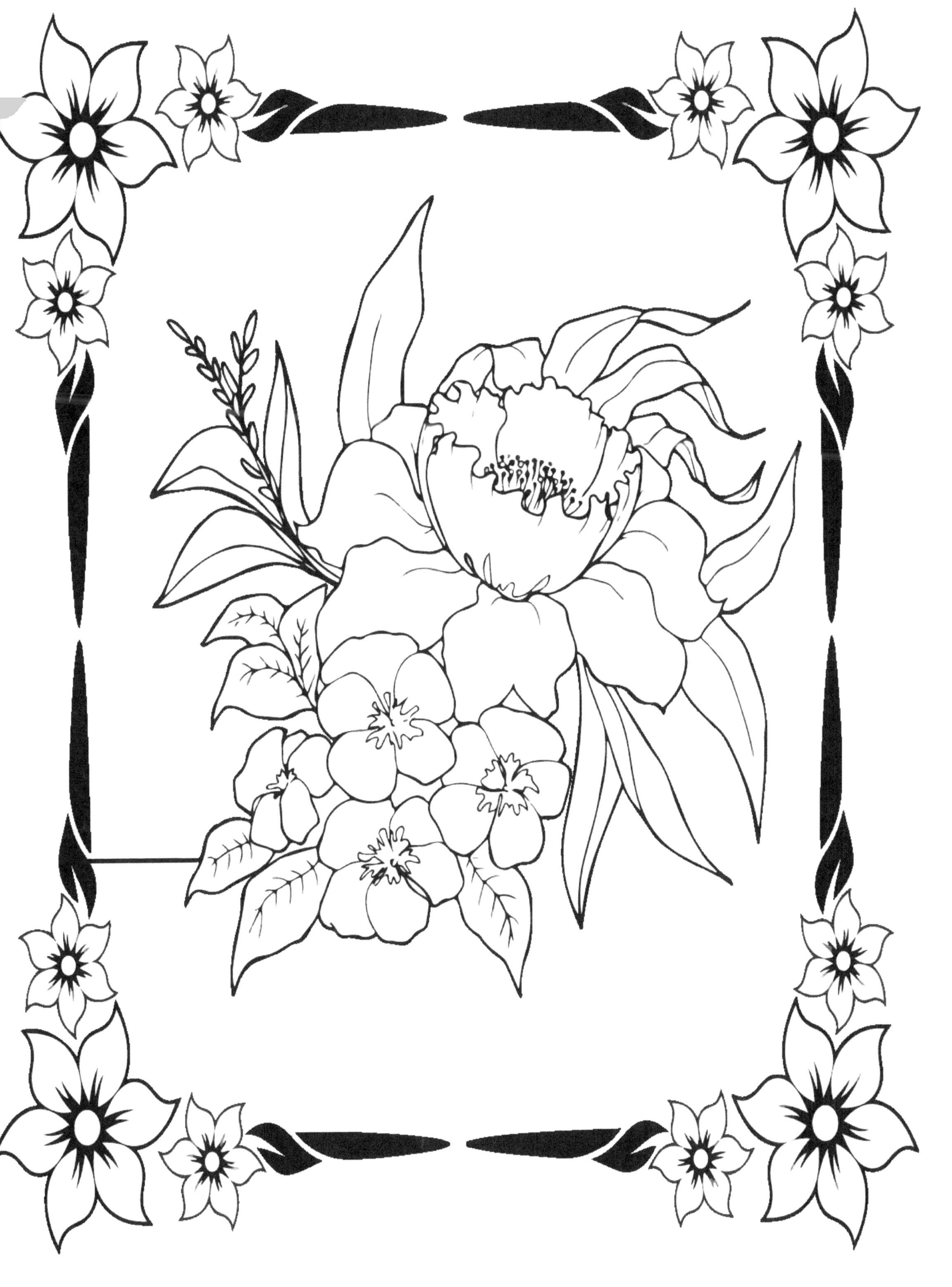

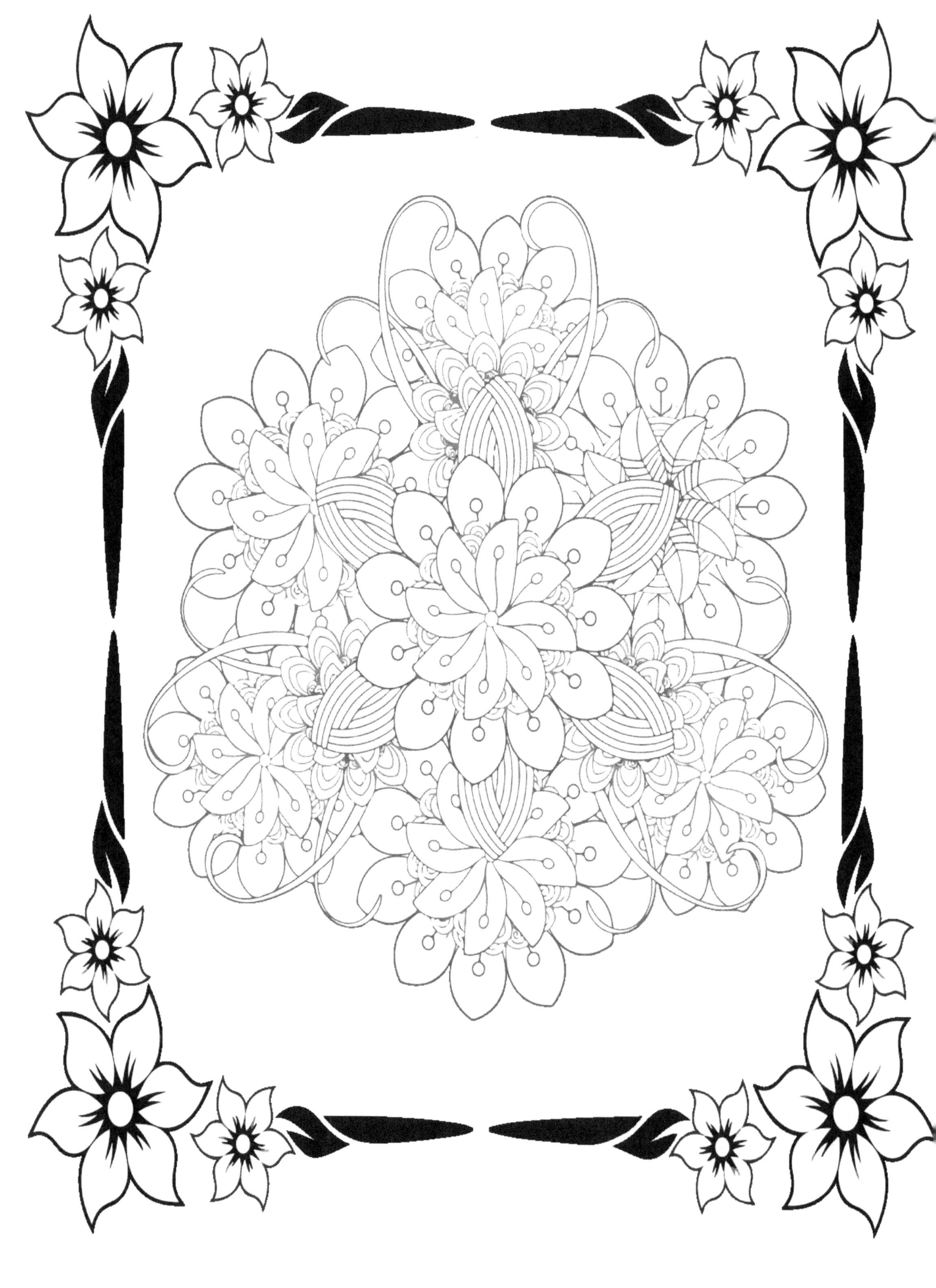

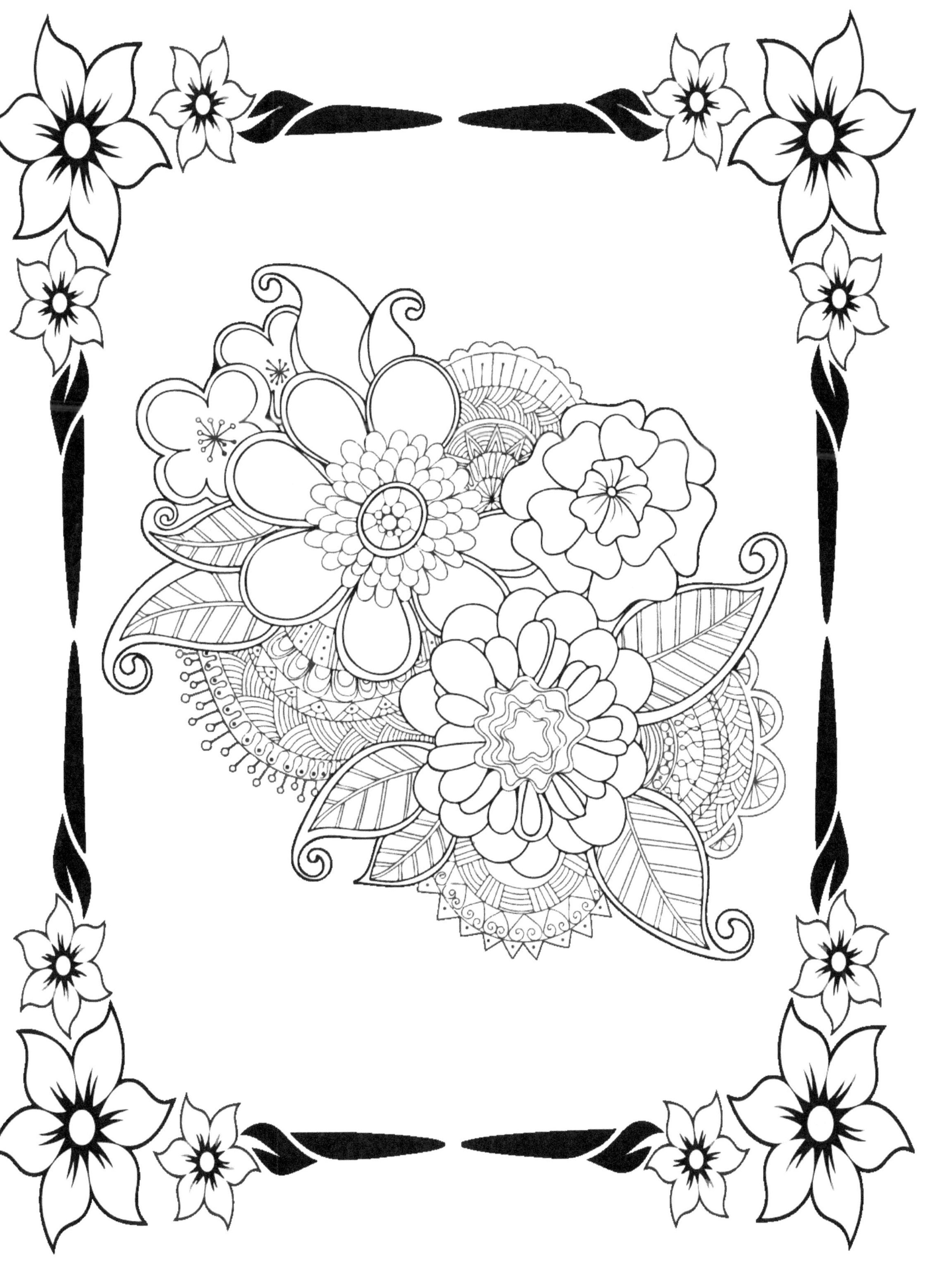

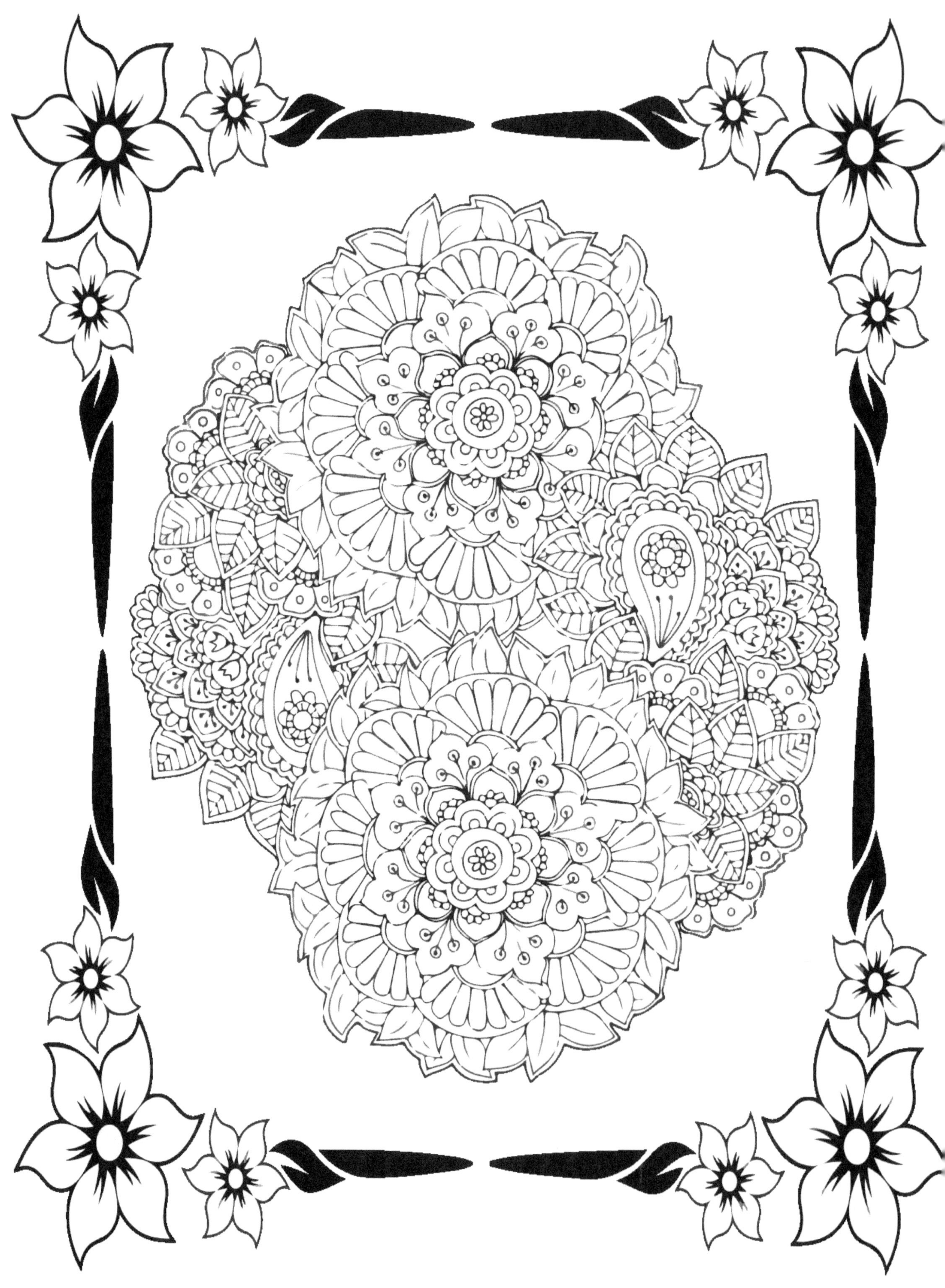

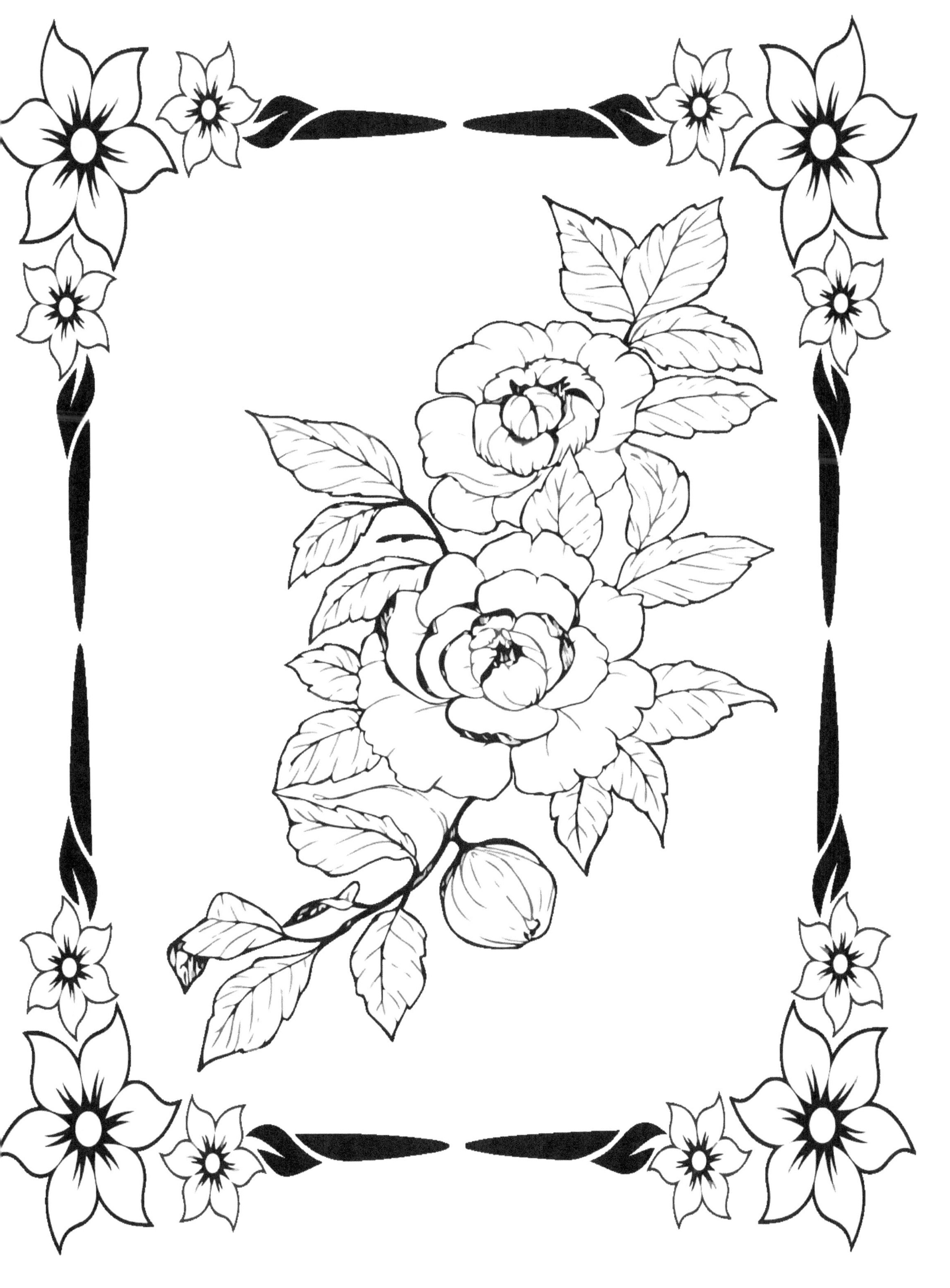

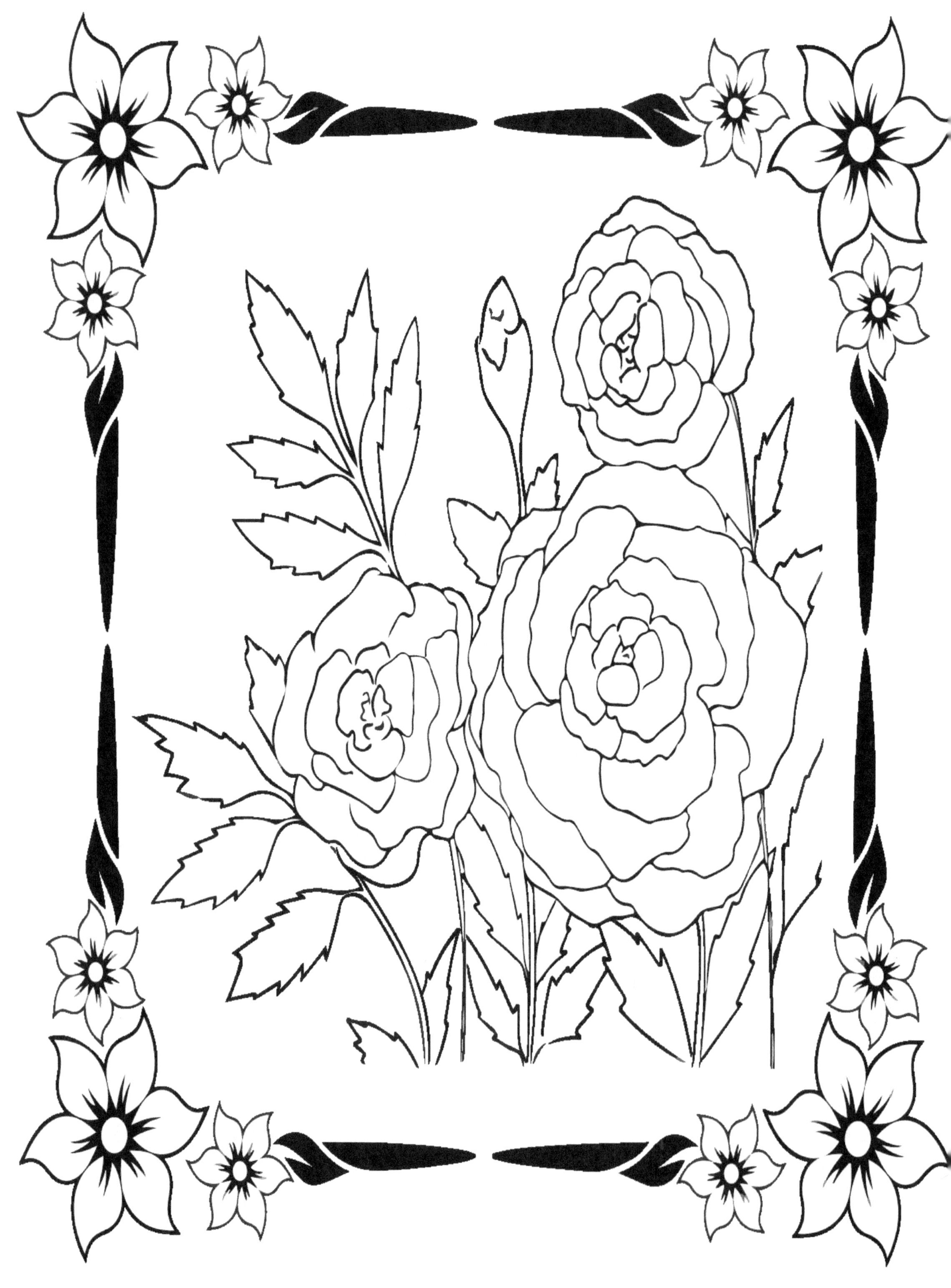

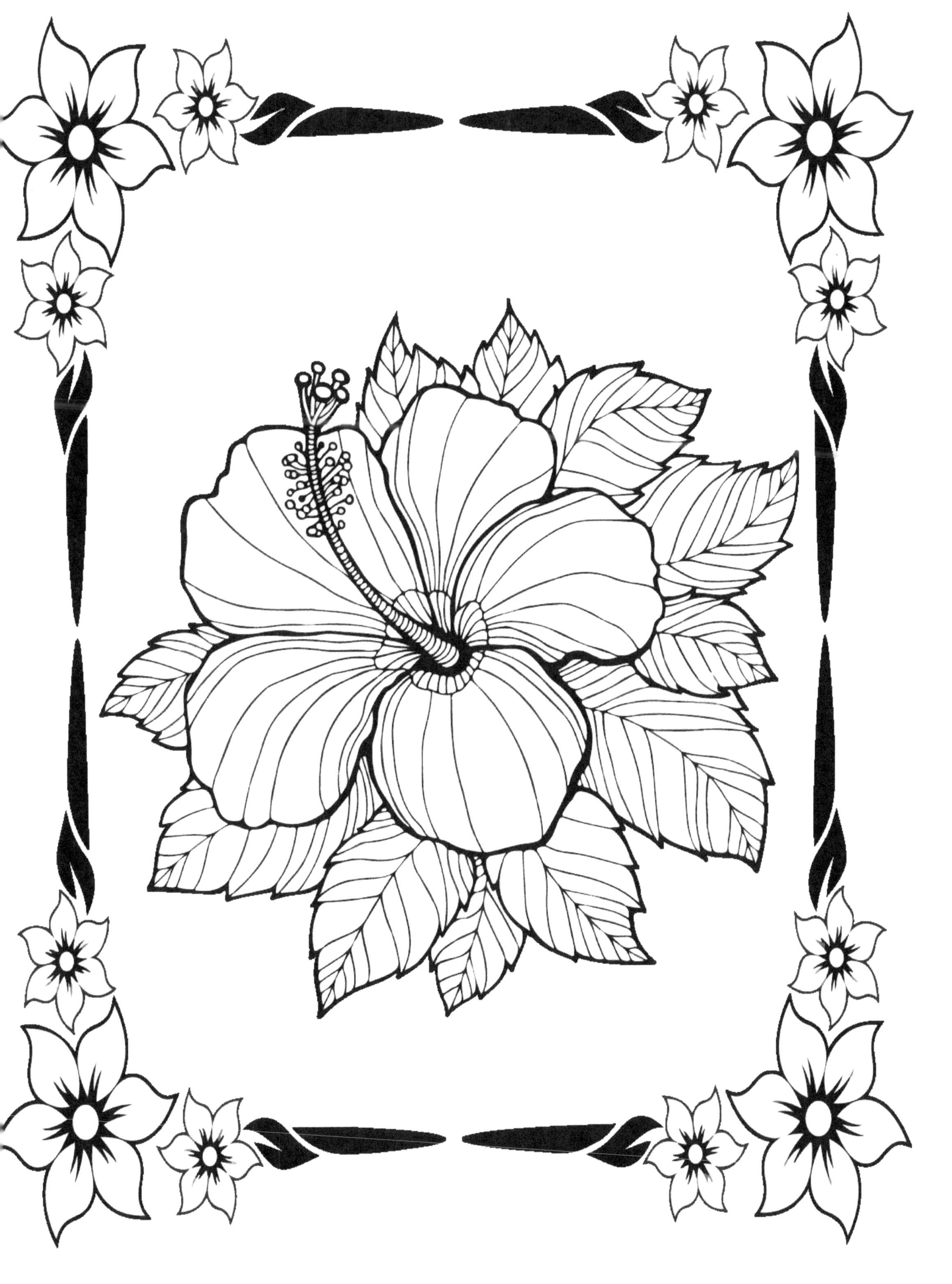

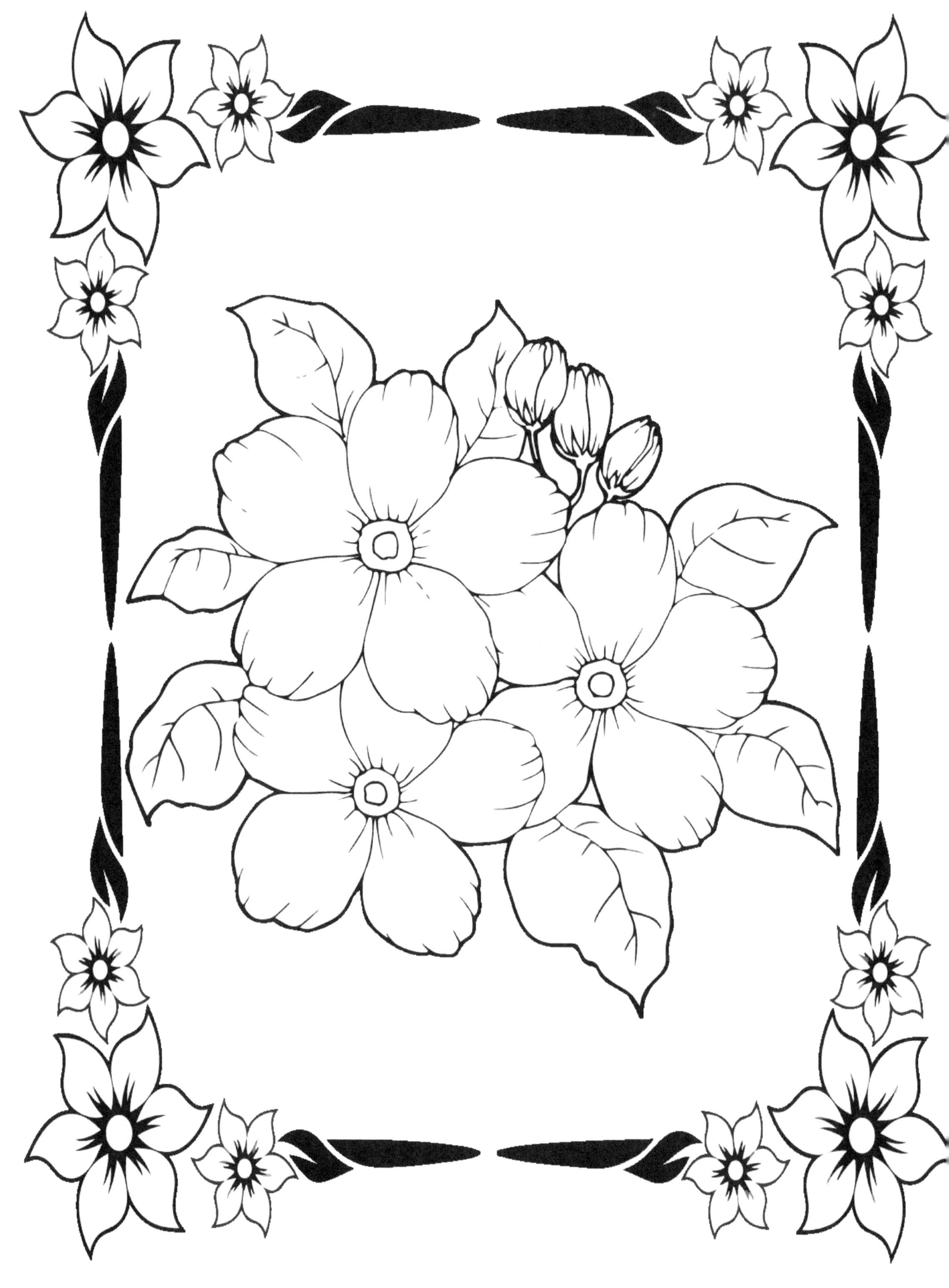

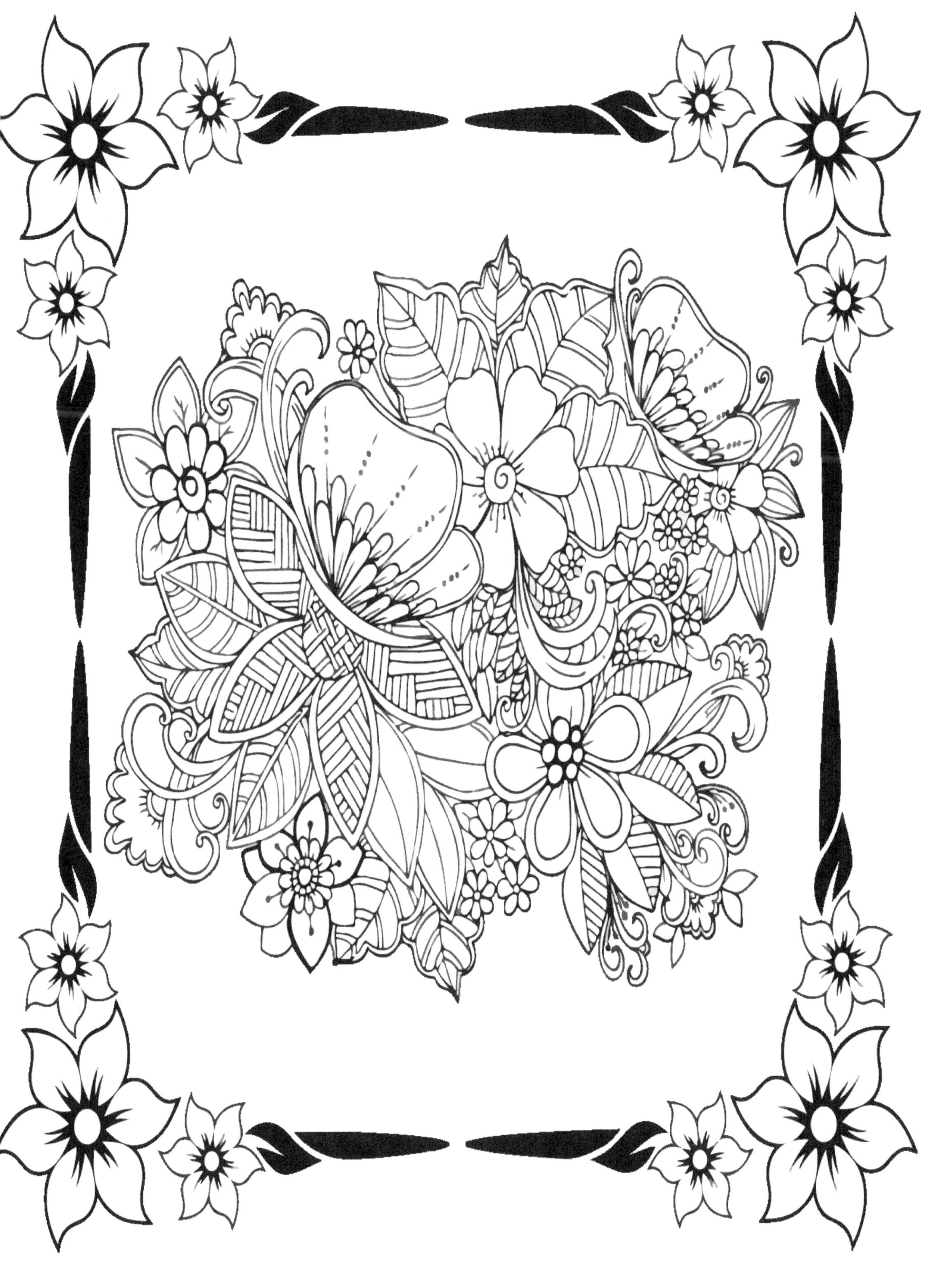

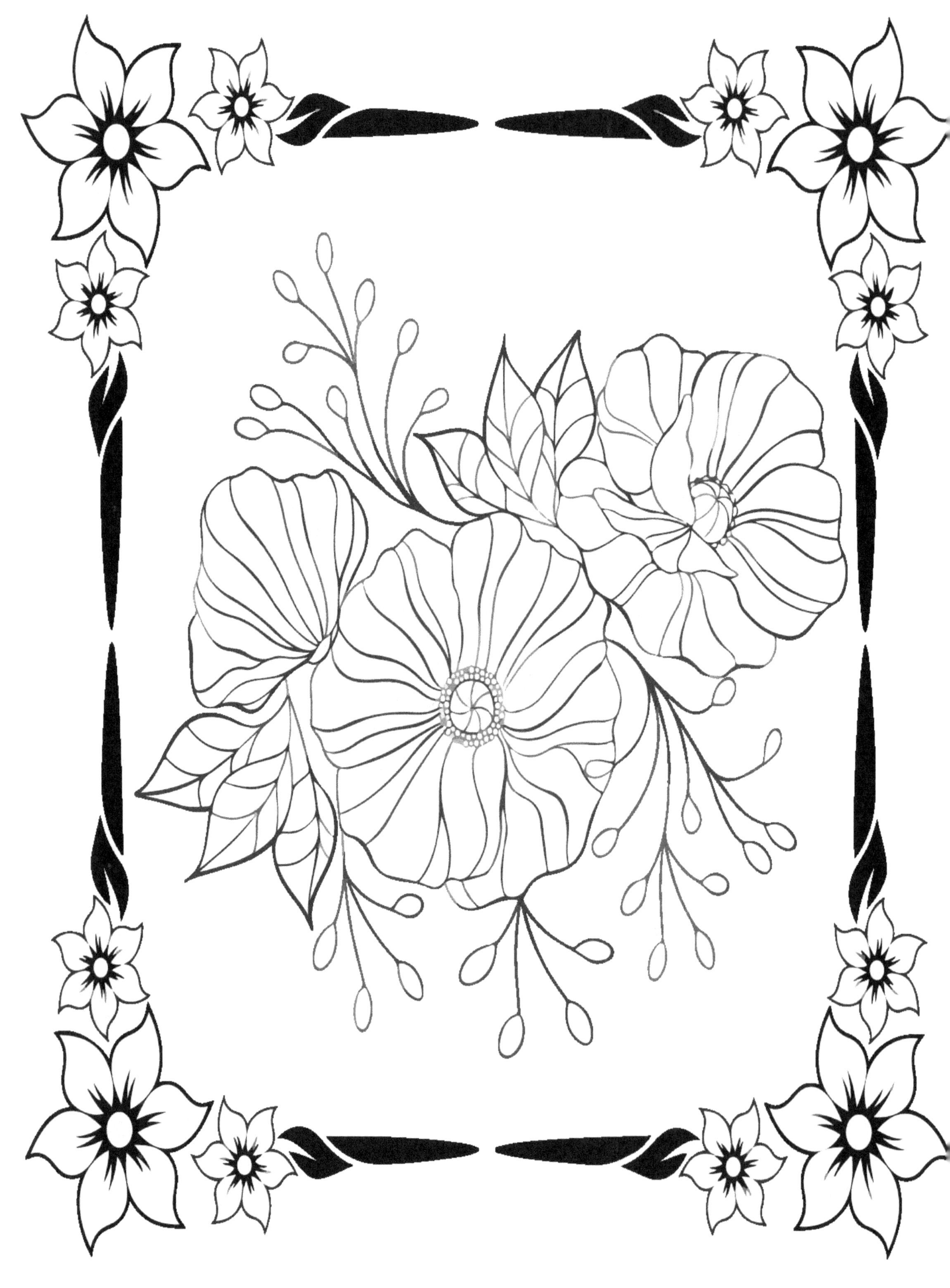

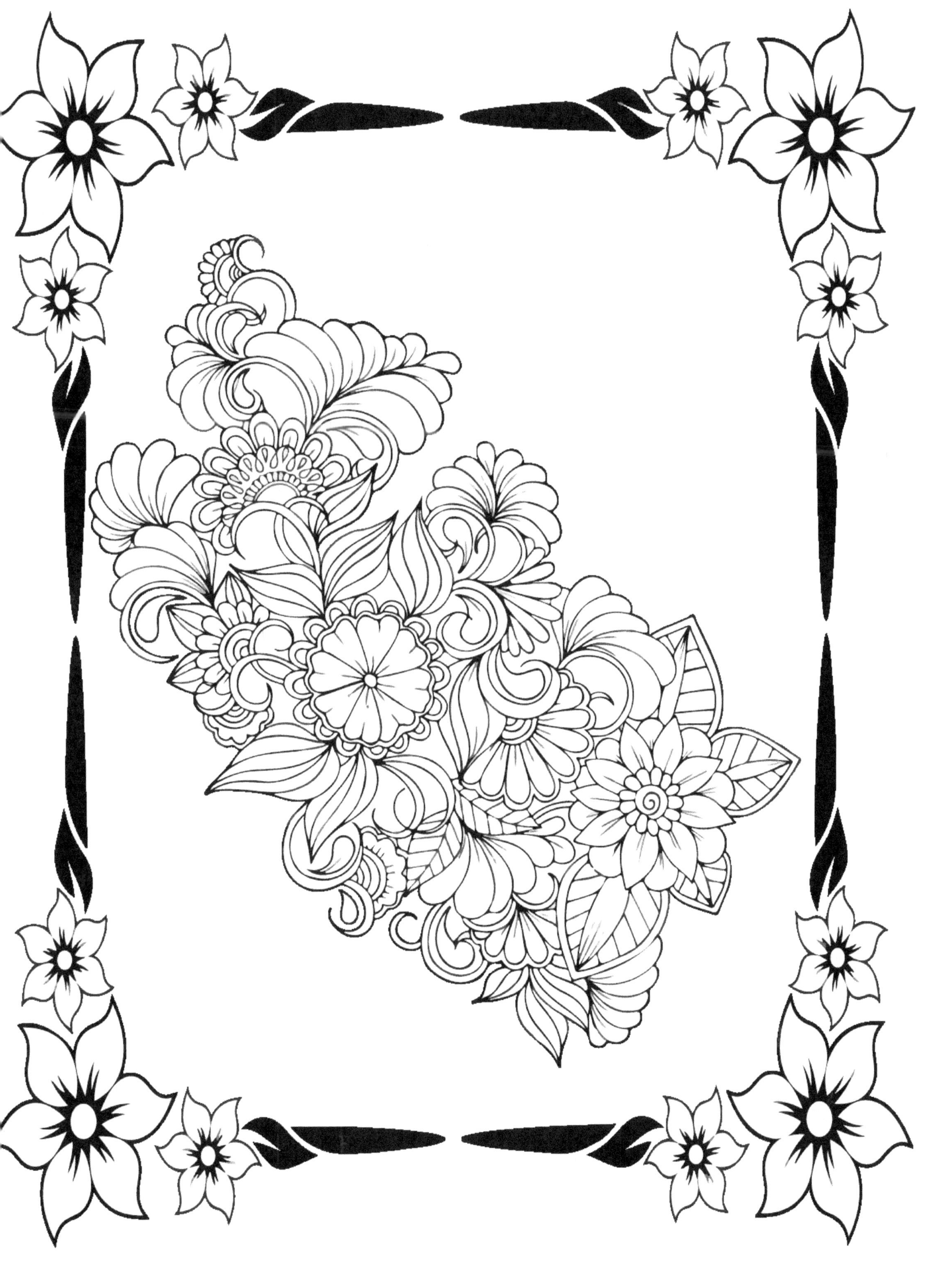

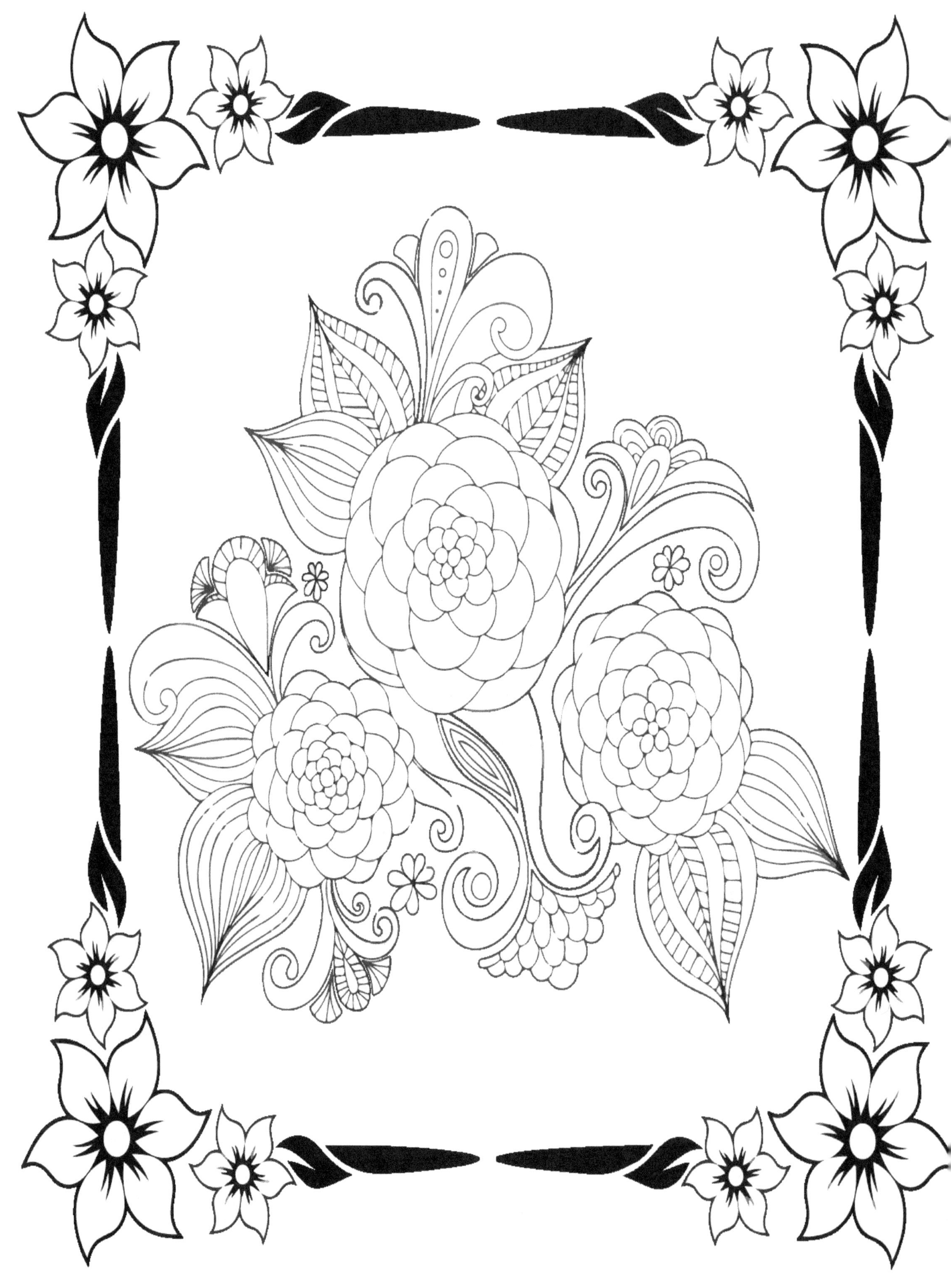

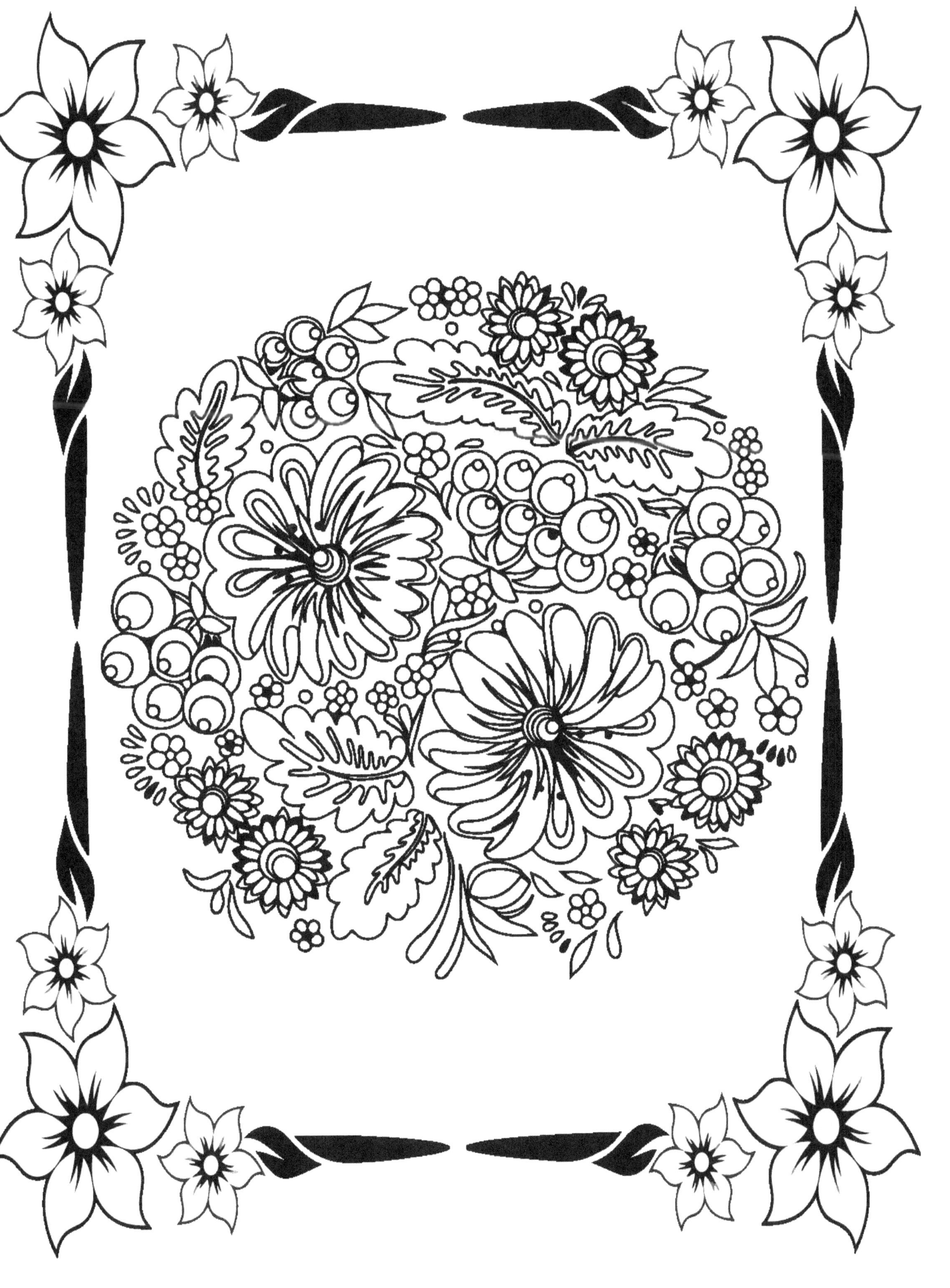

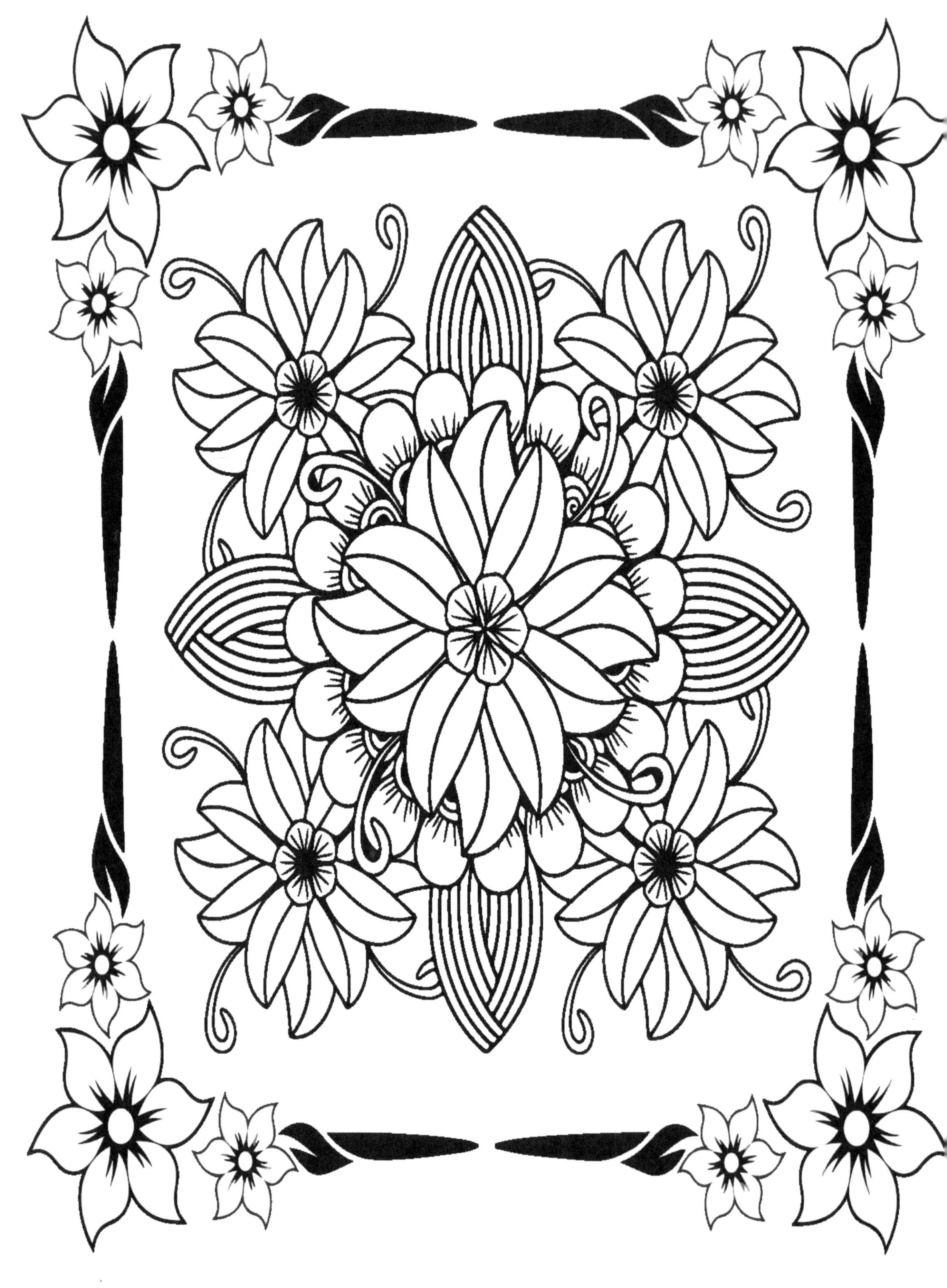

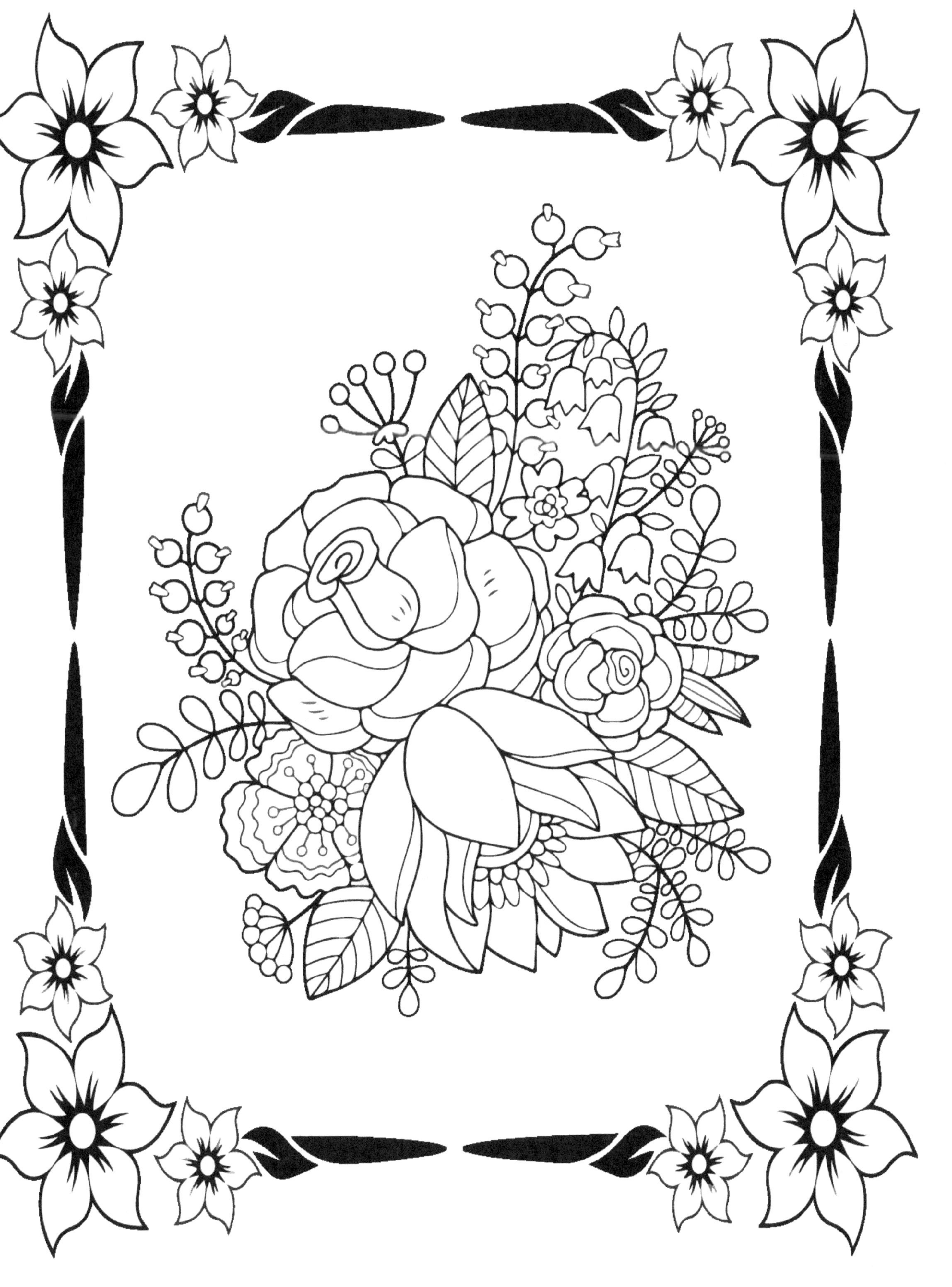

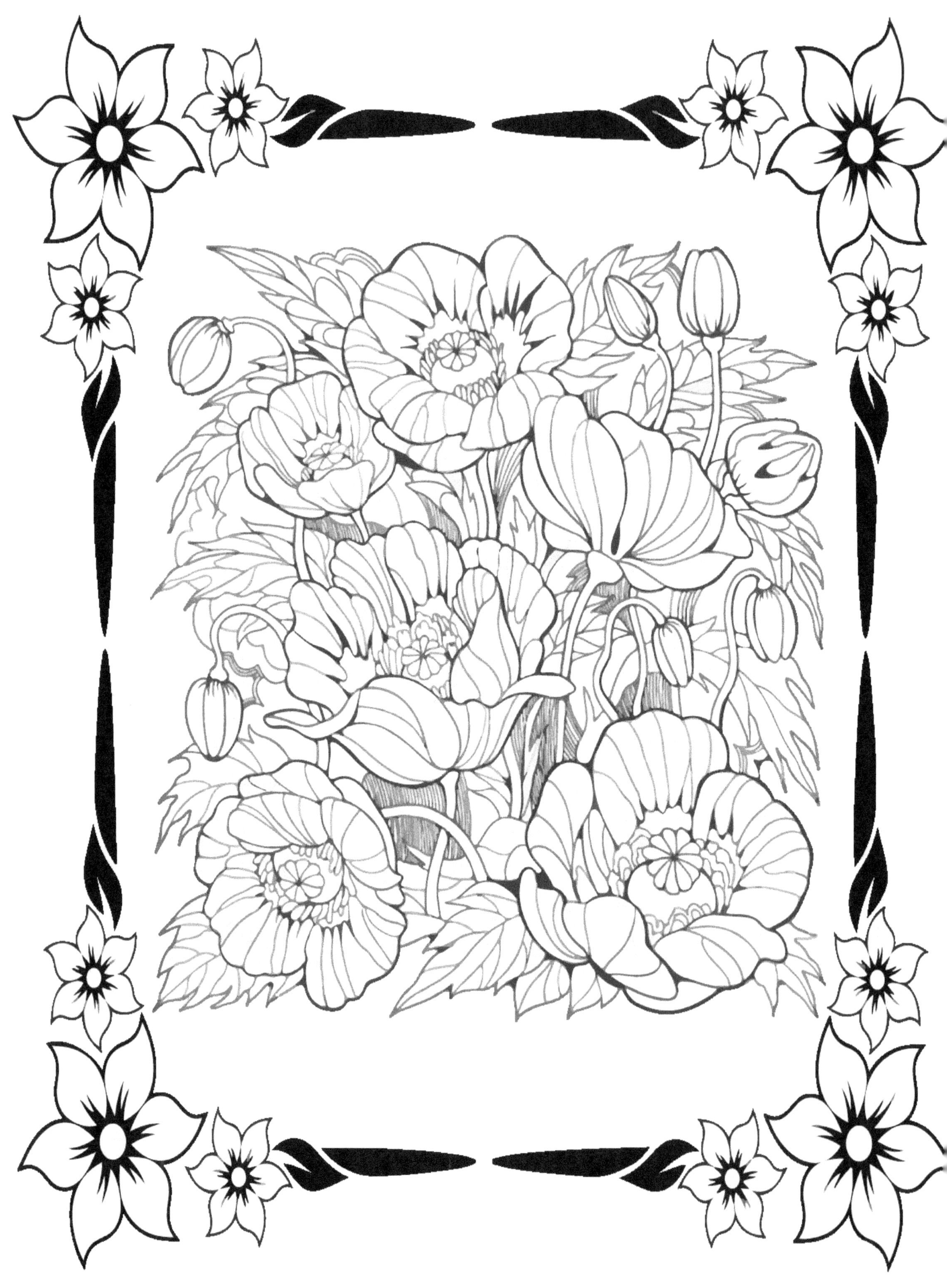

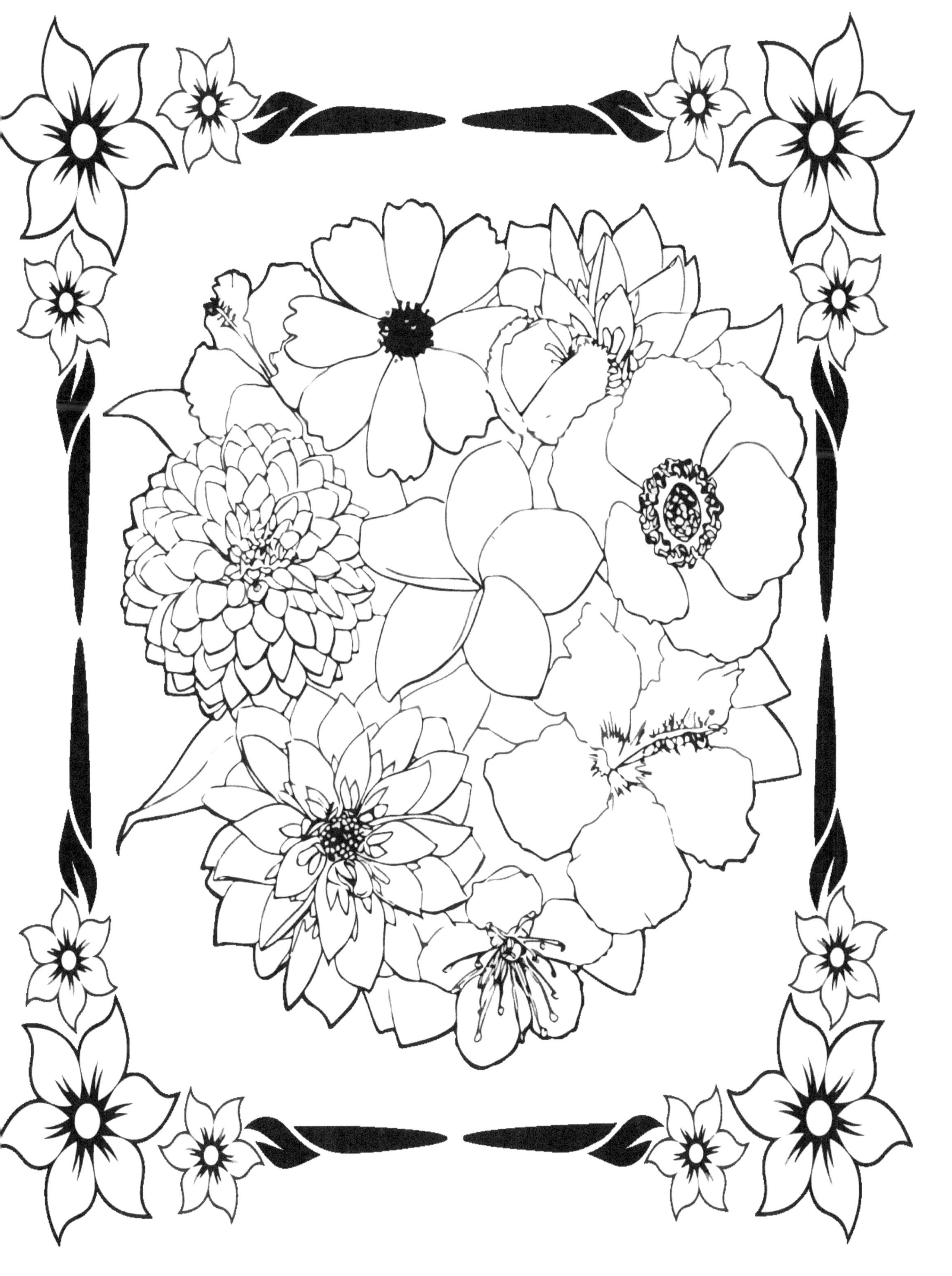

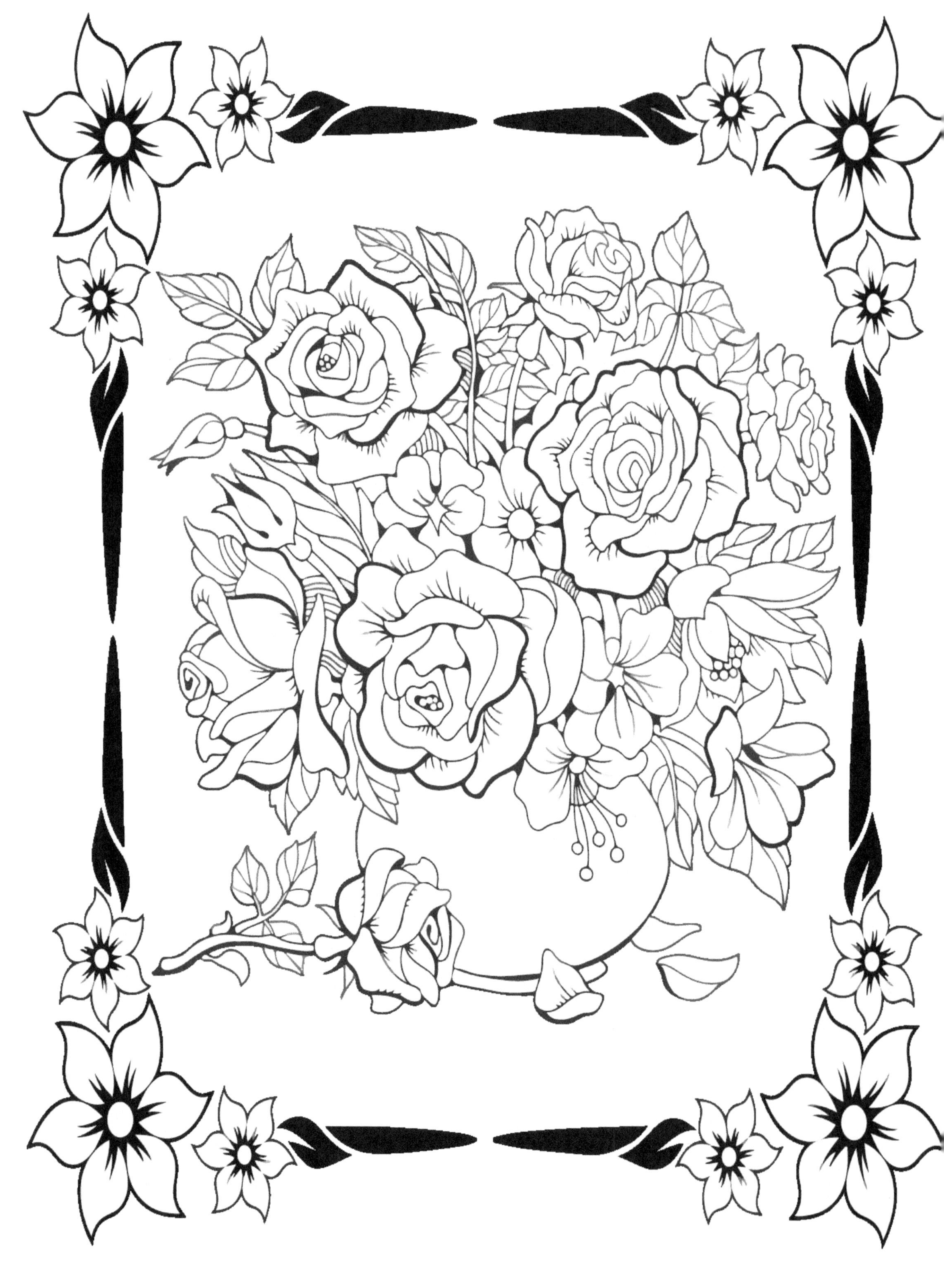

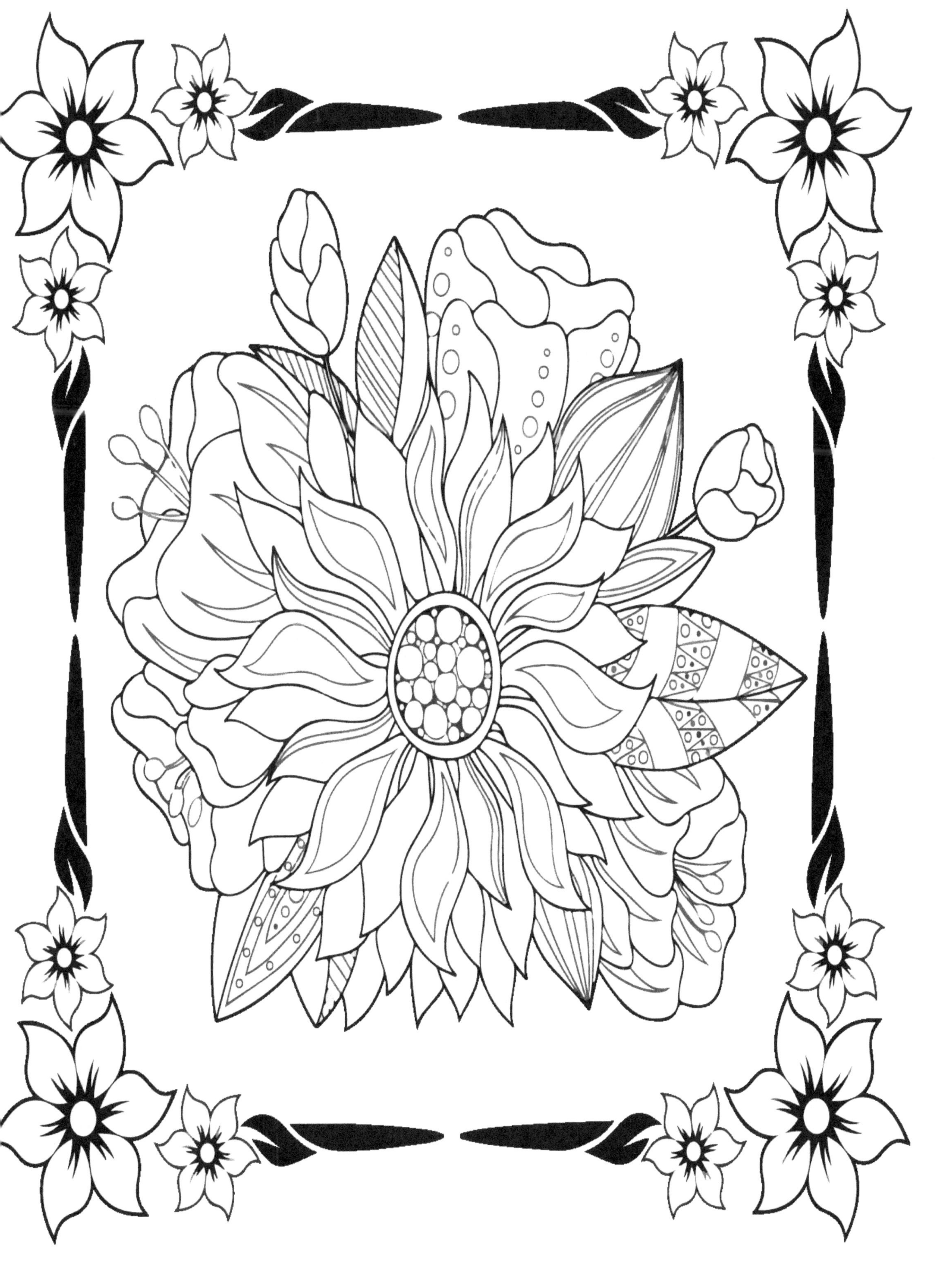

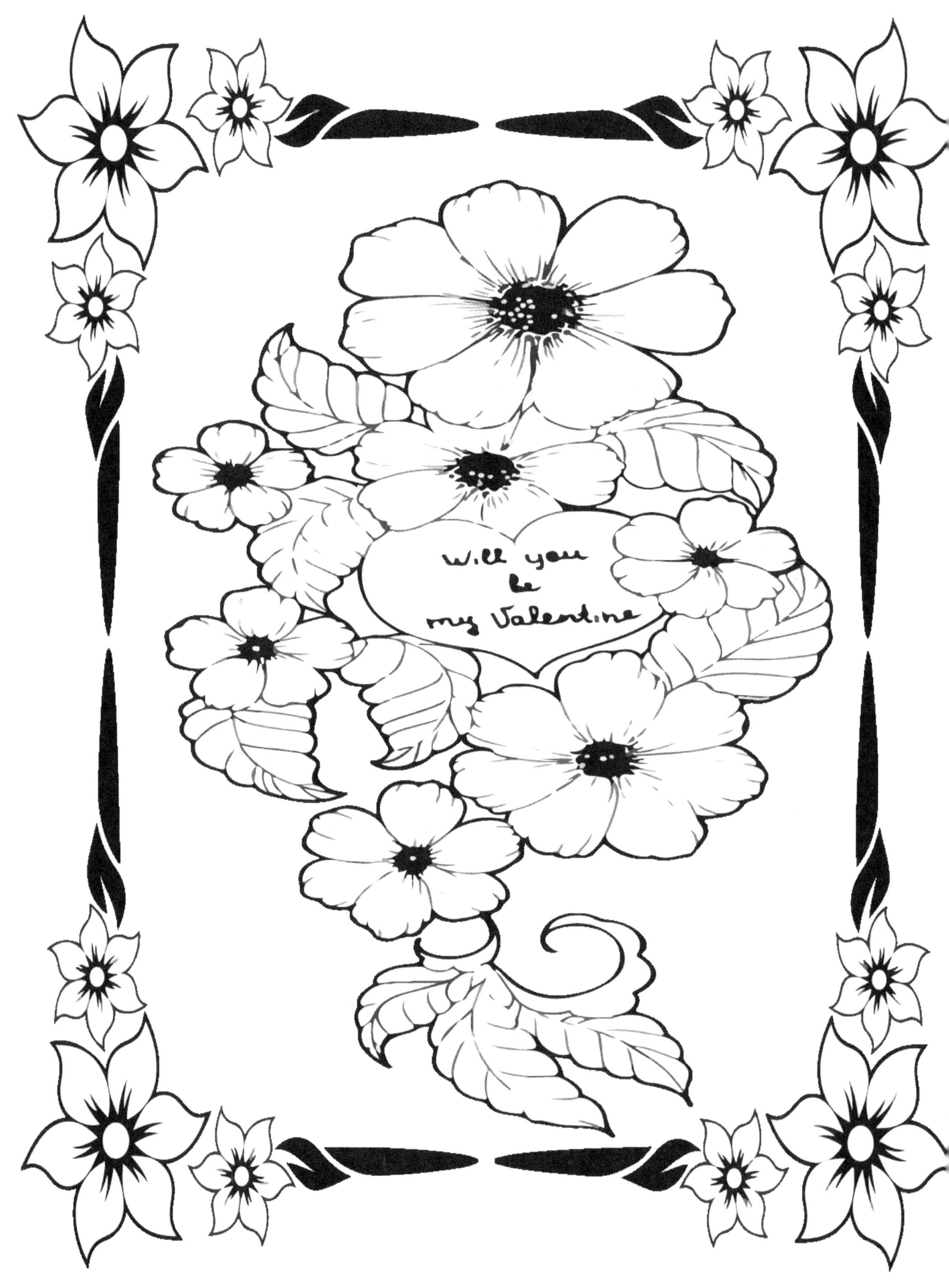
will you
be
my Valentine

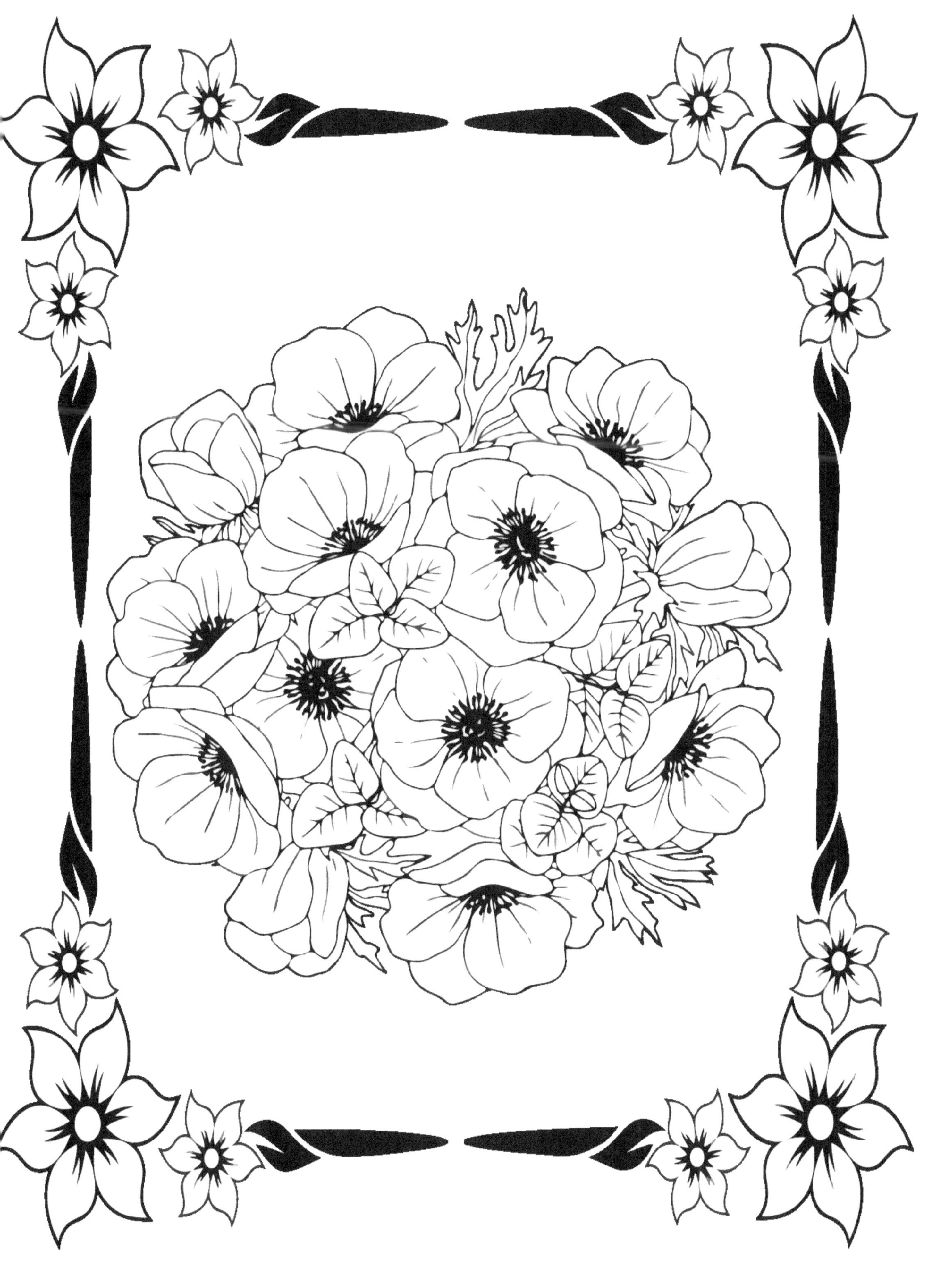

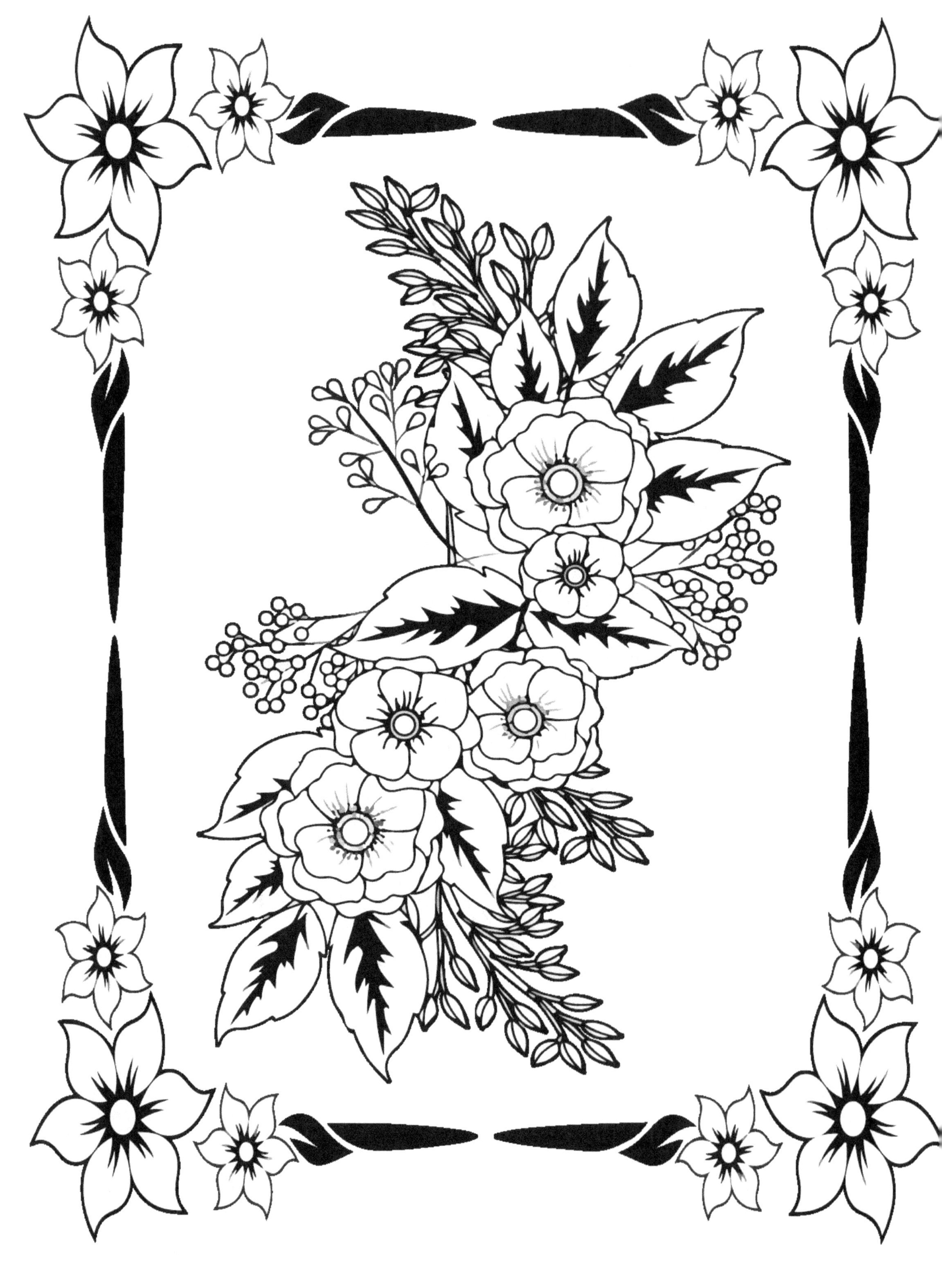

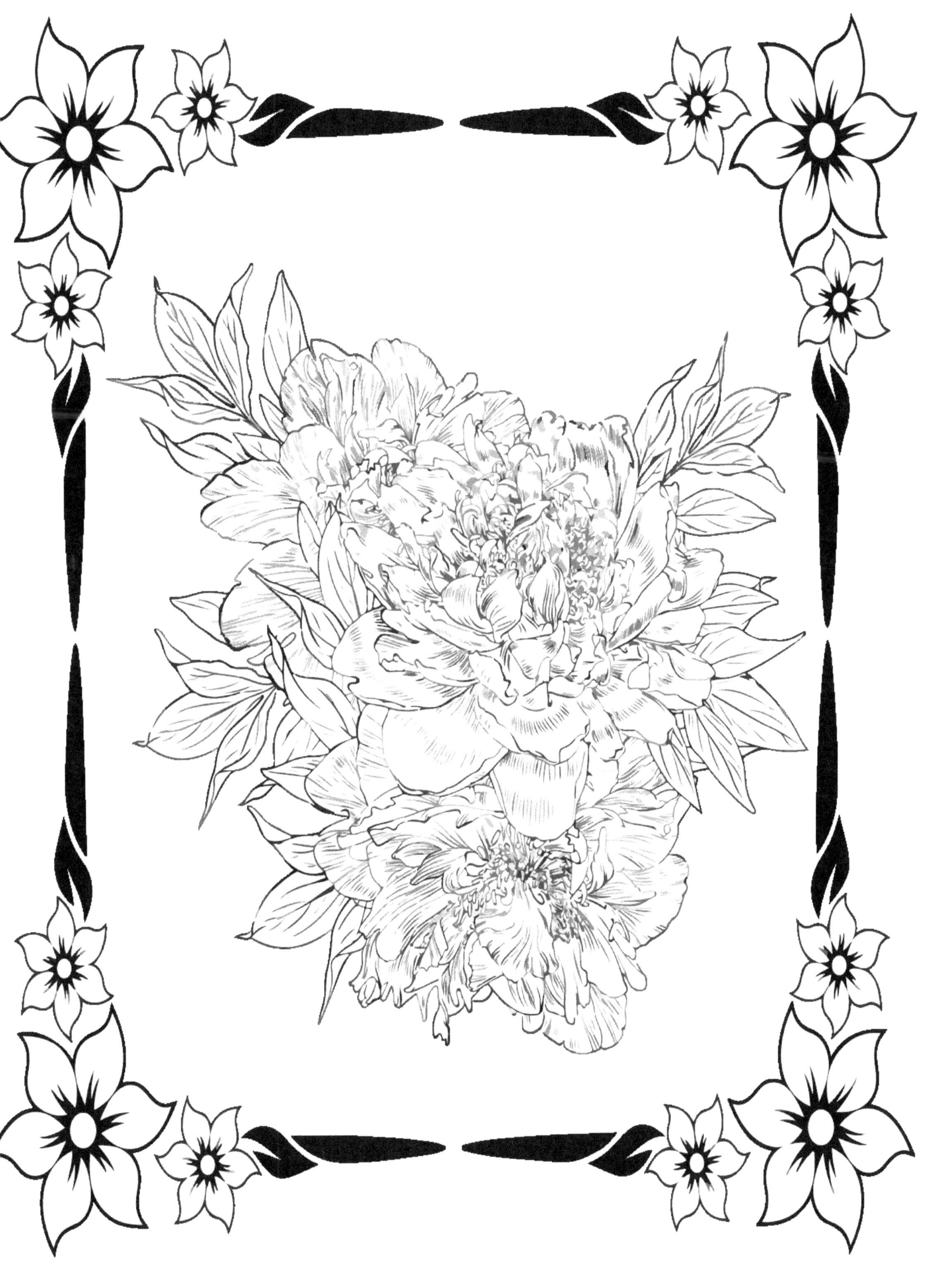

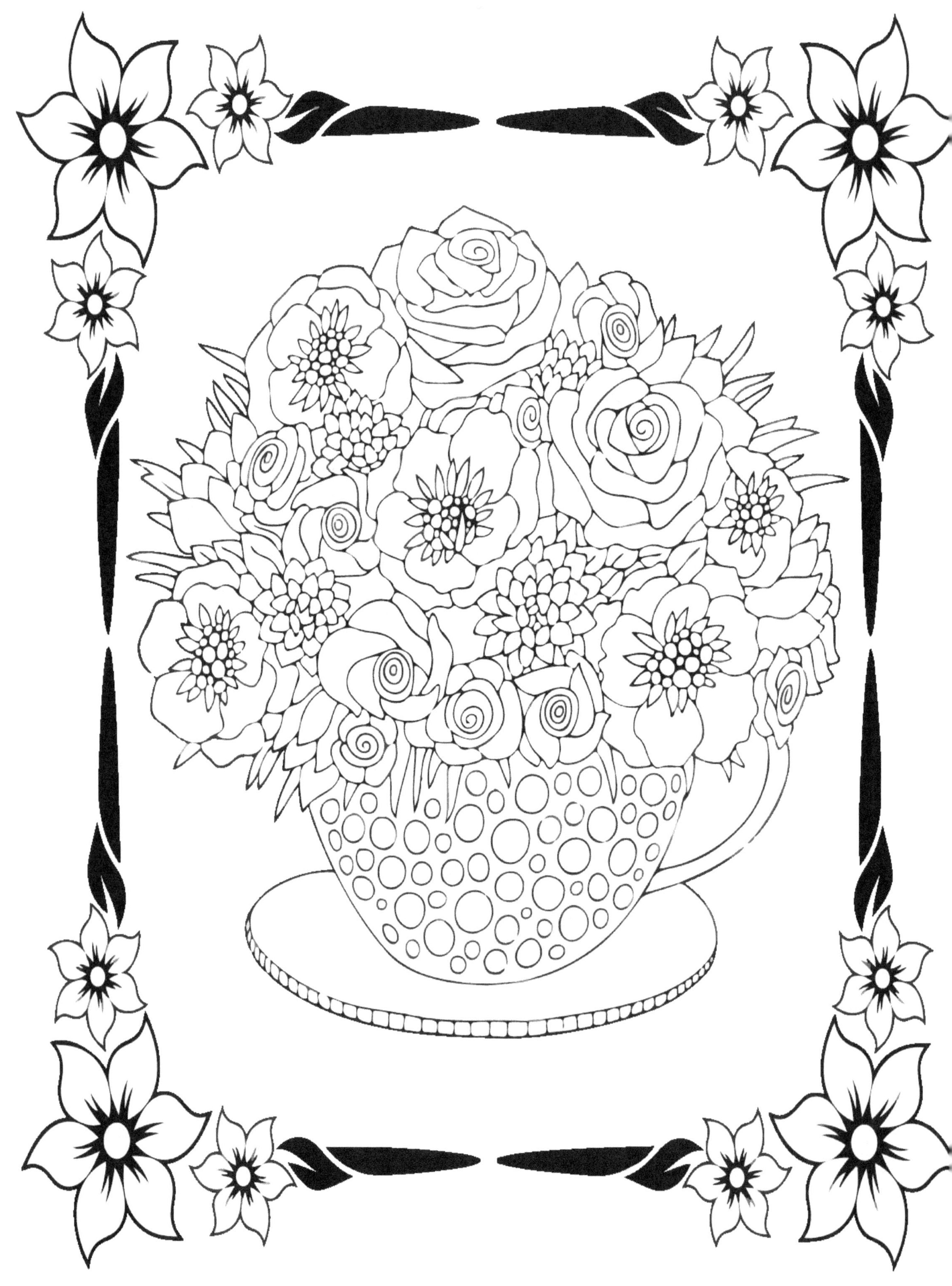

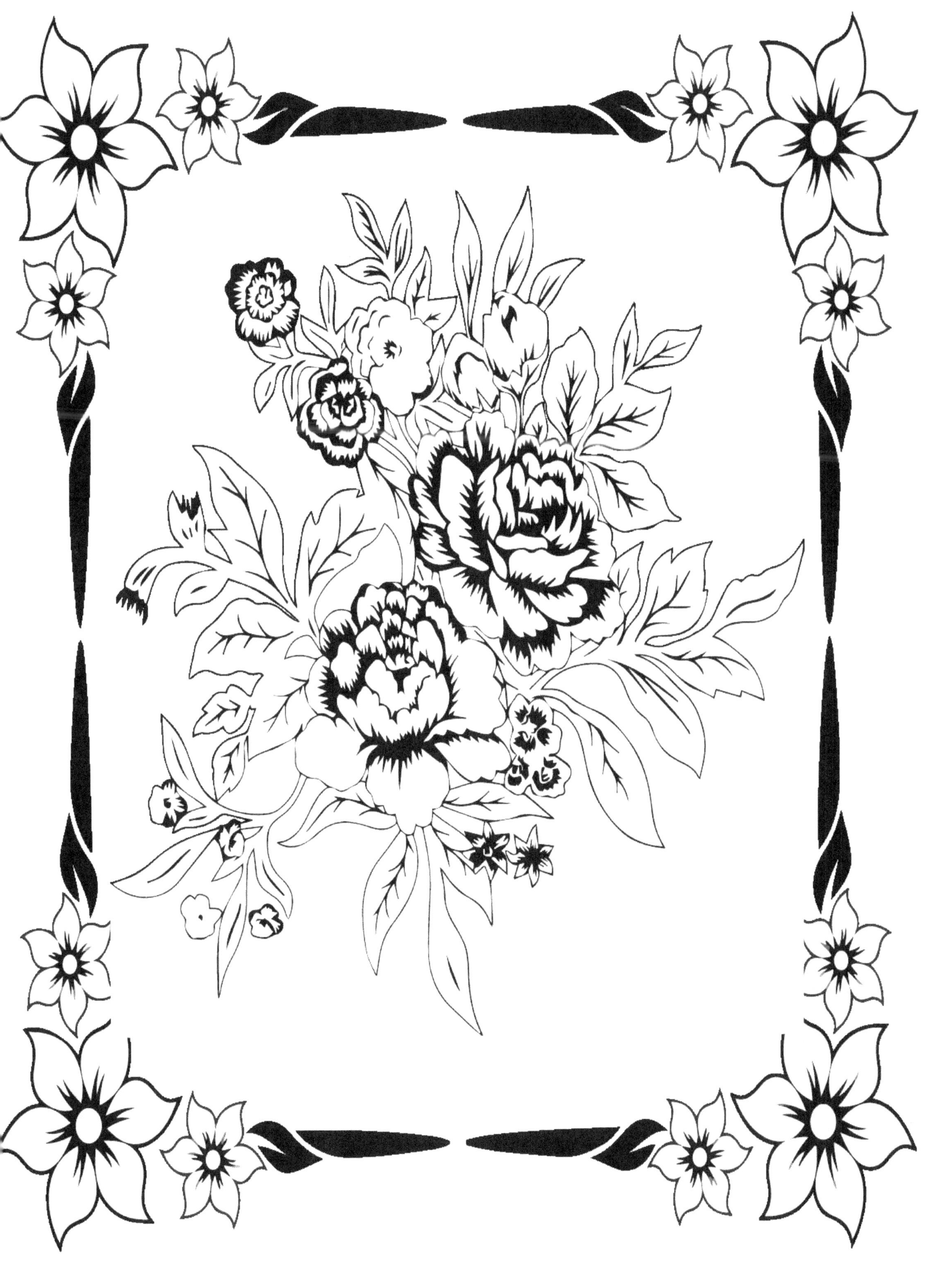

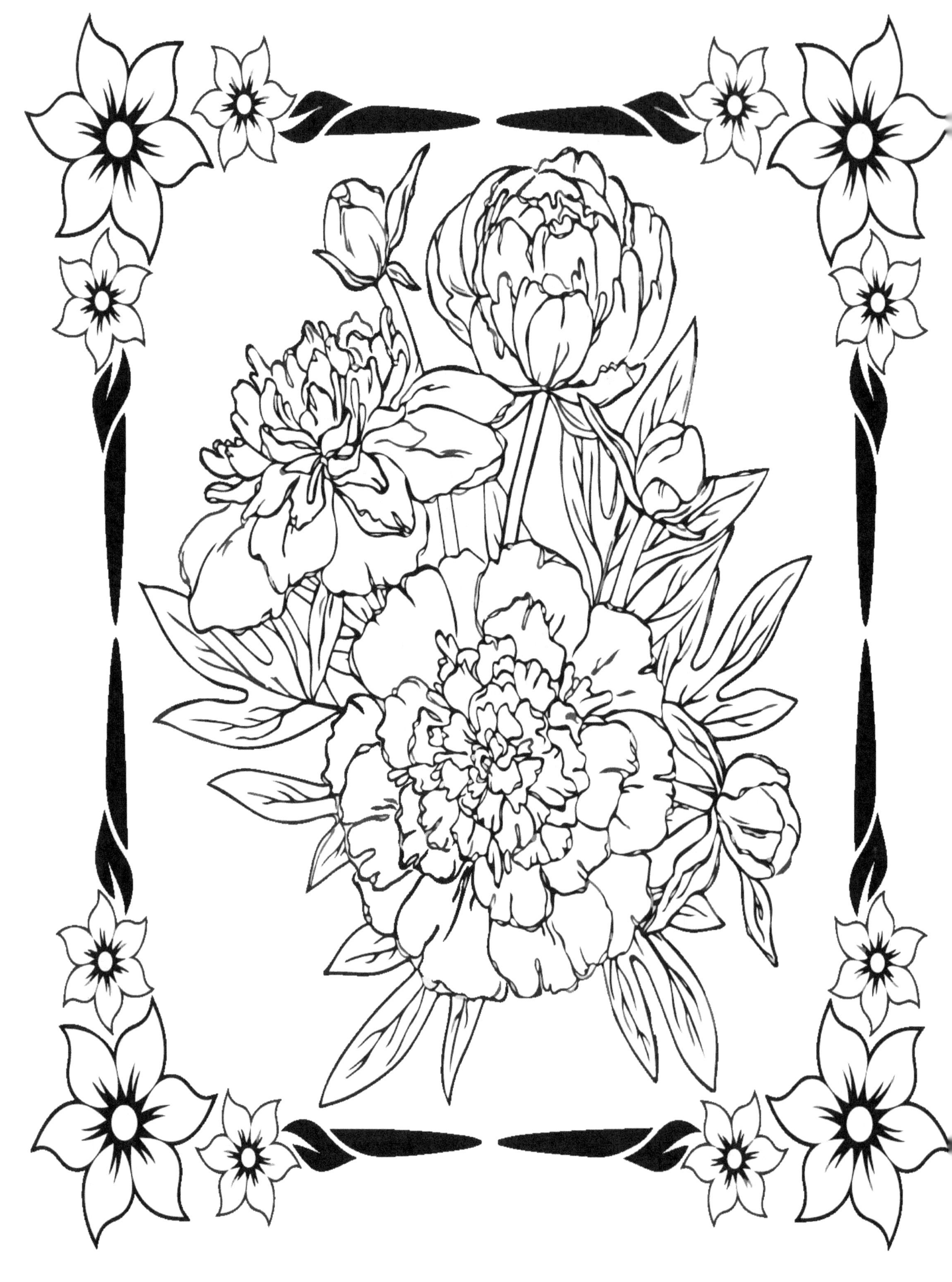

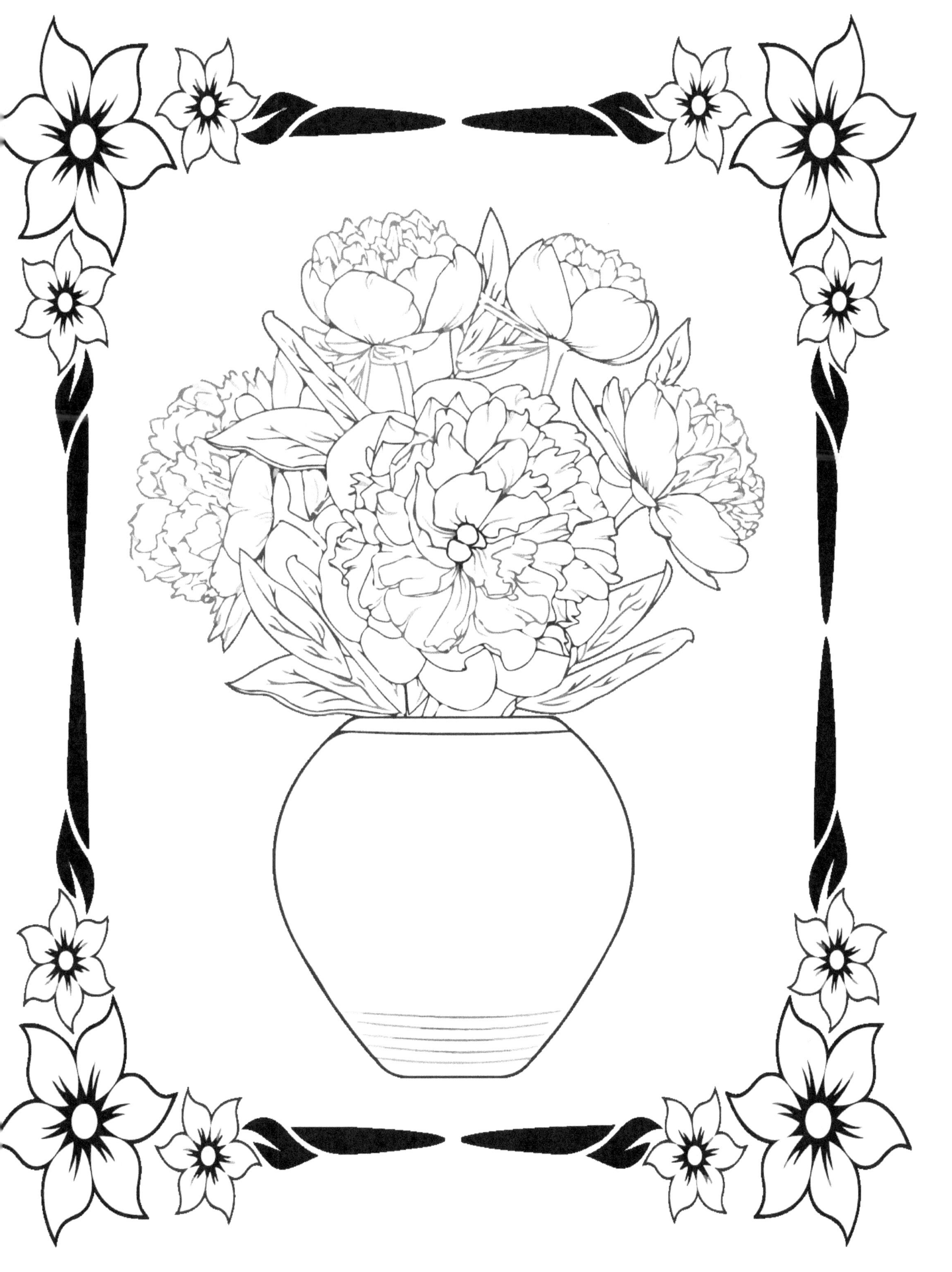

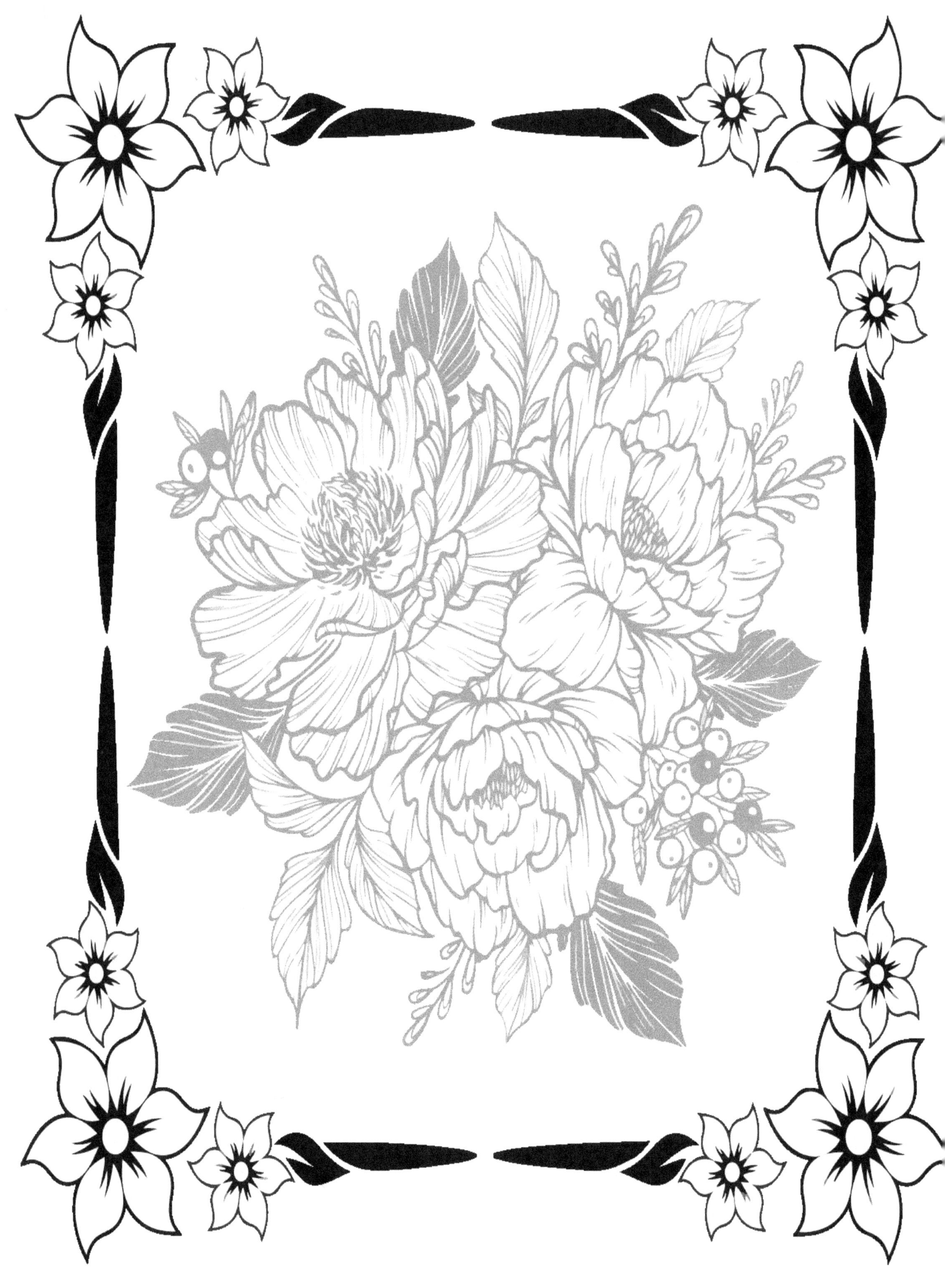

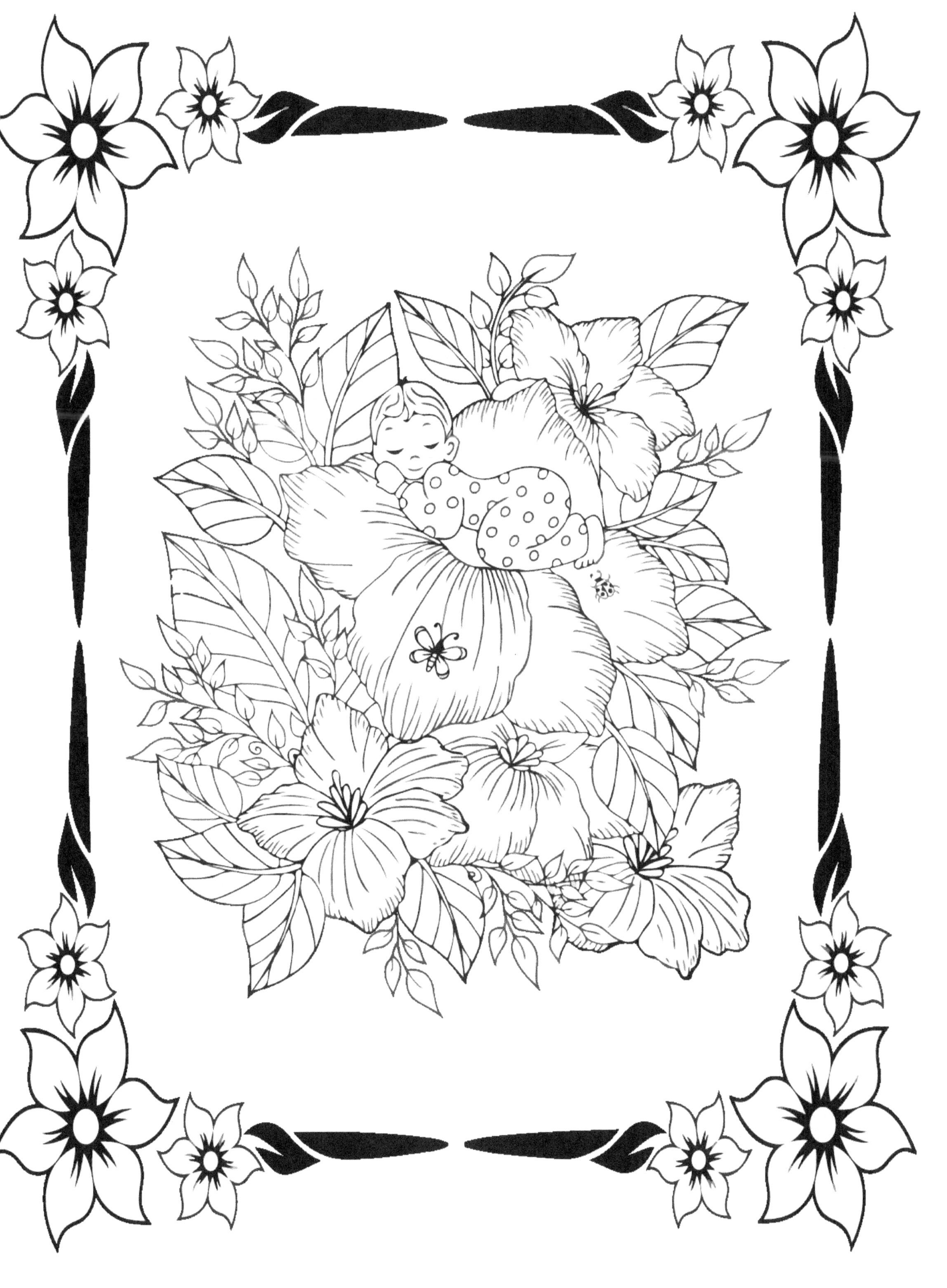

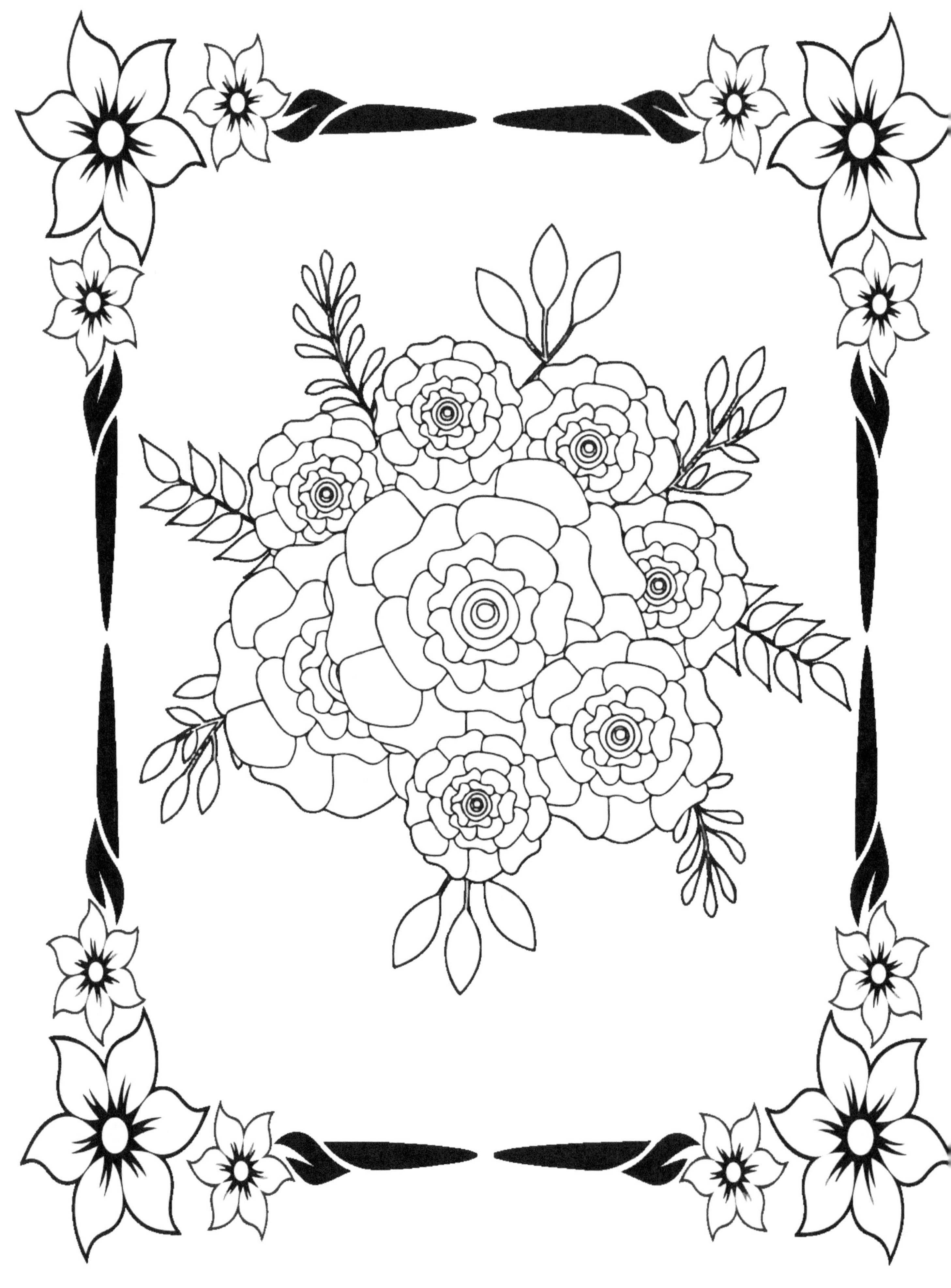

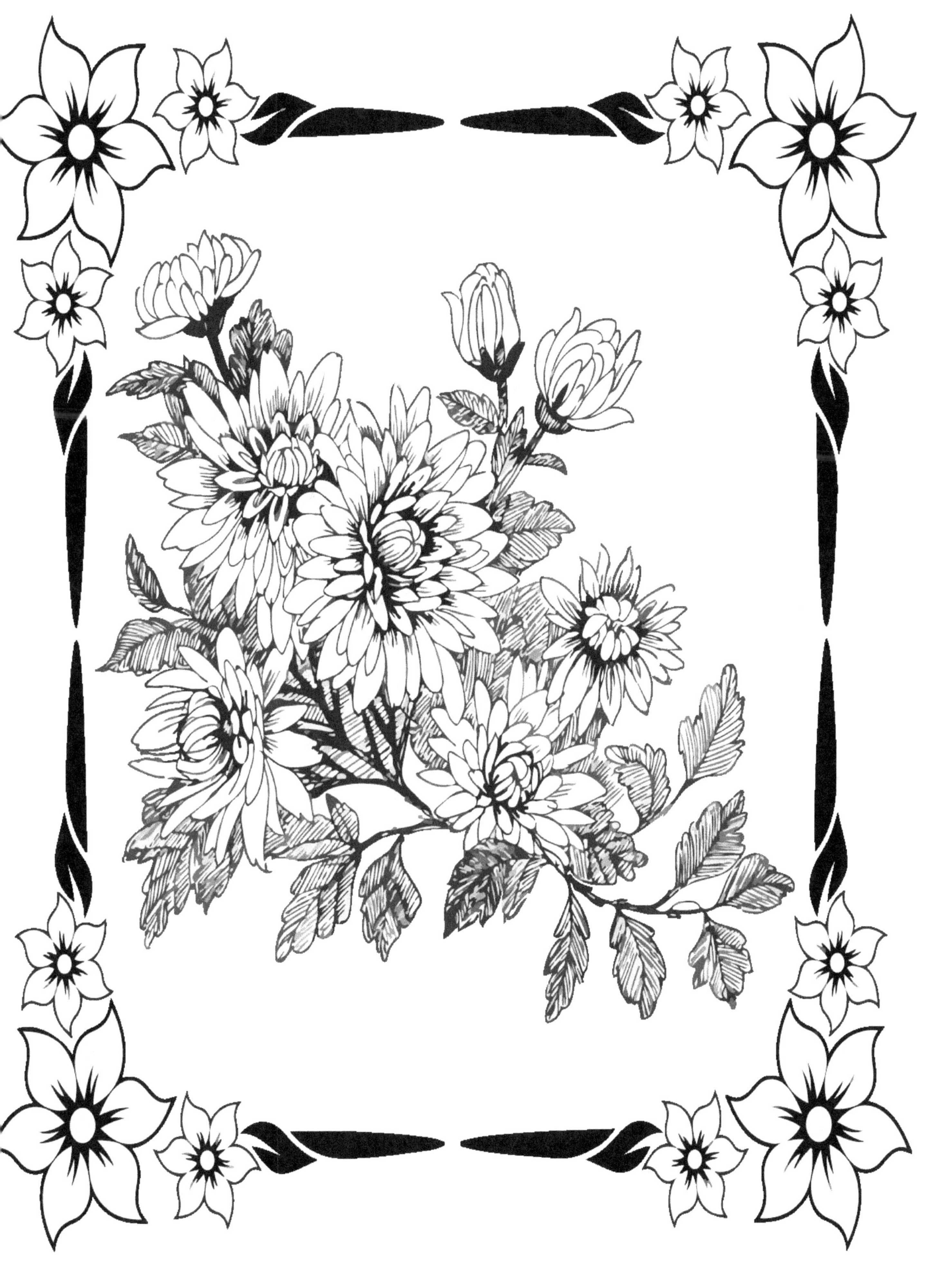

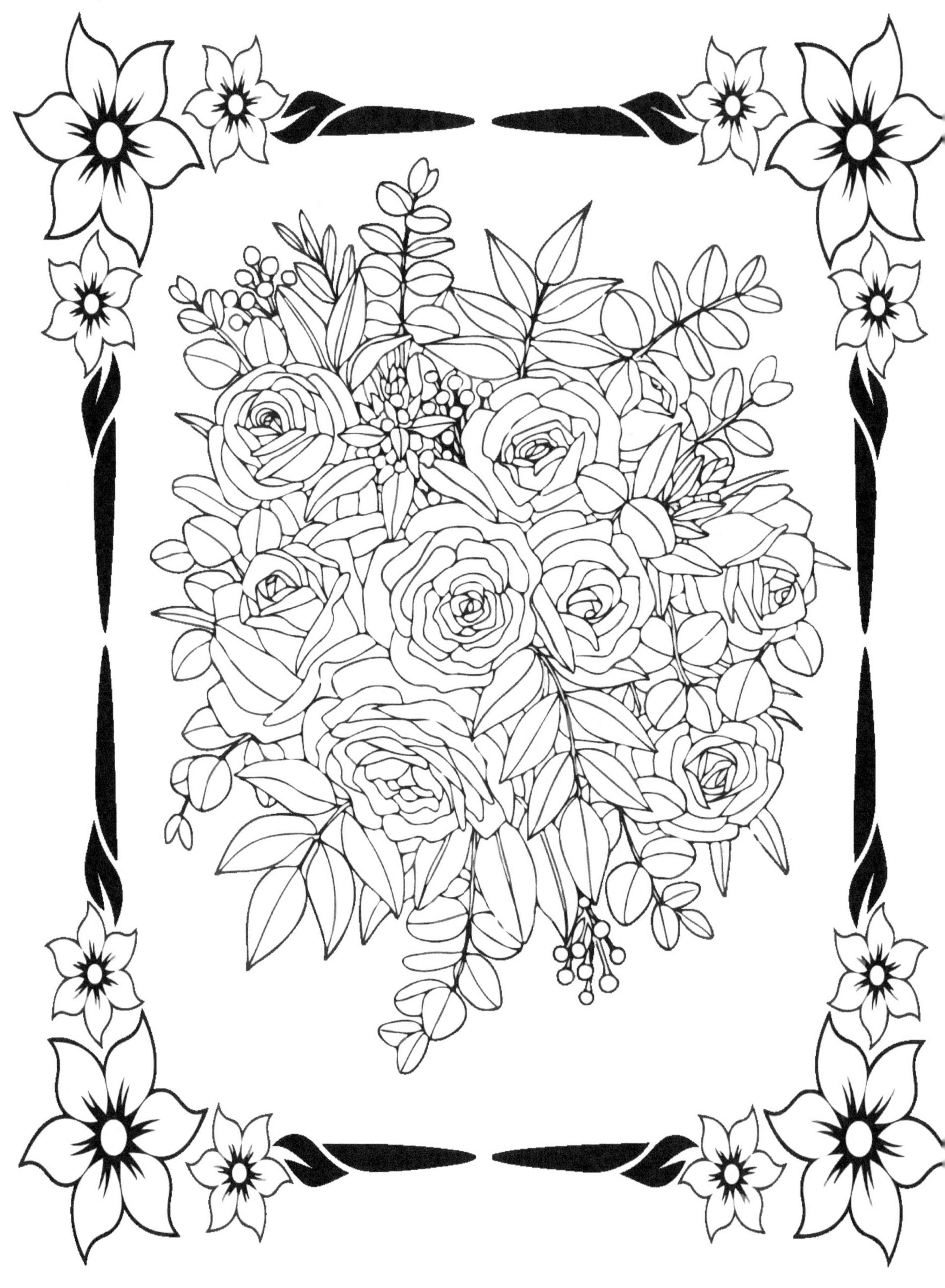

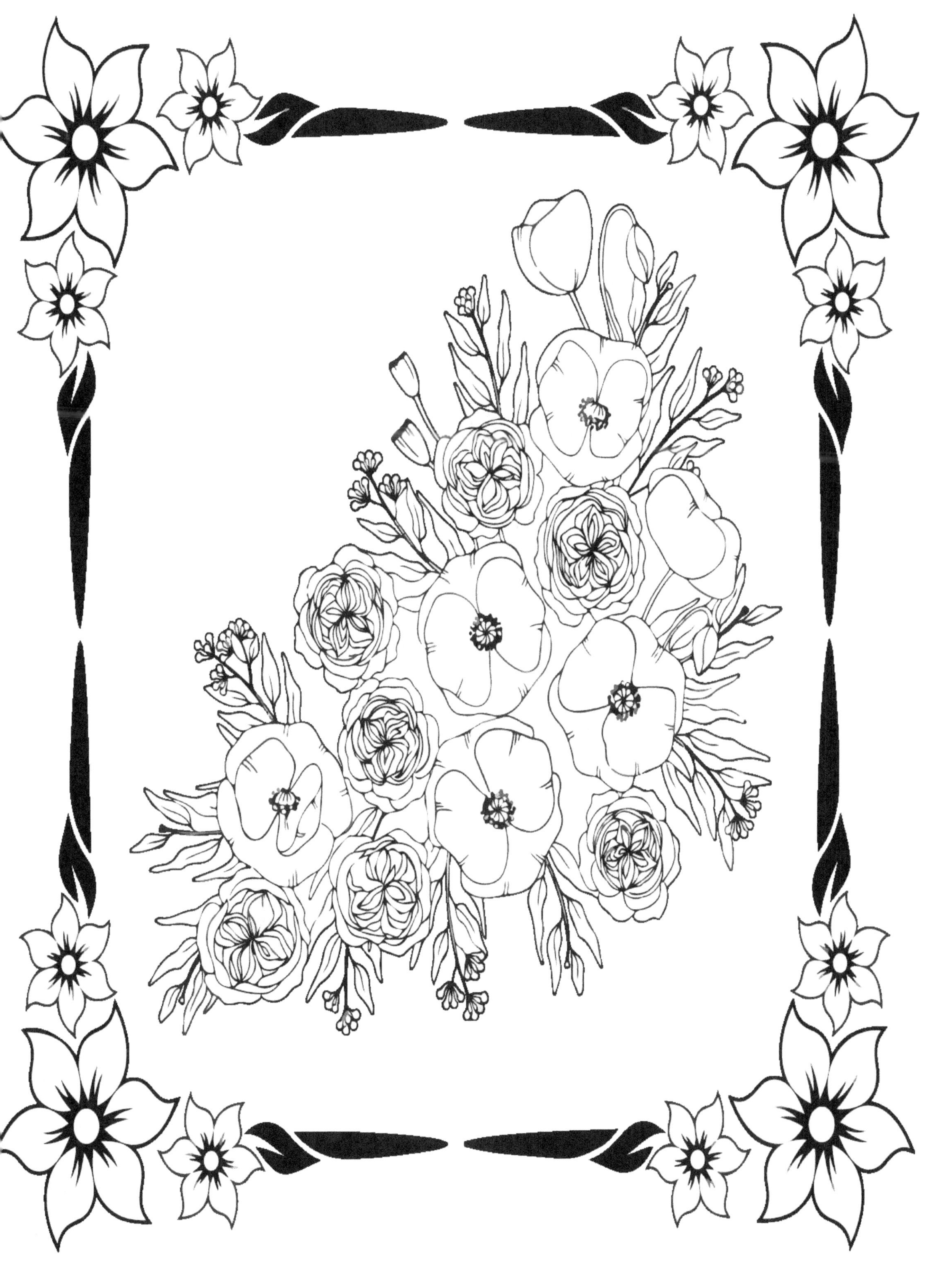

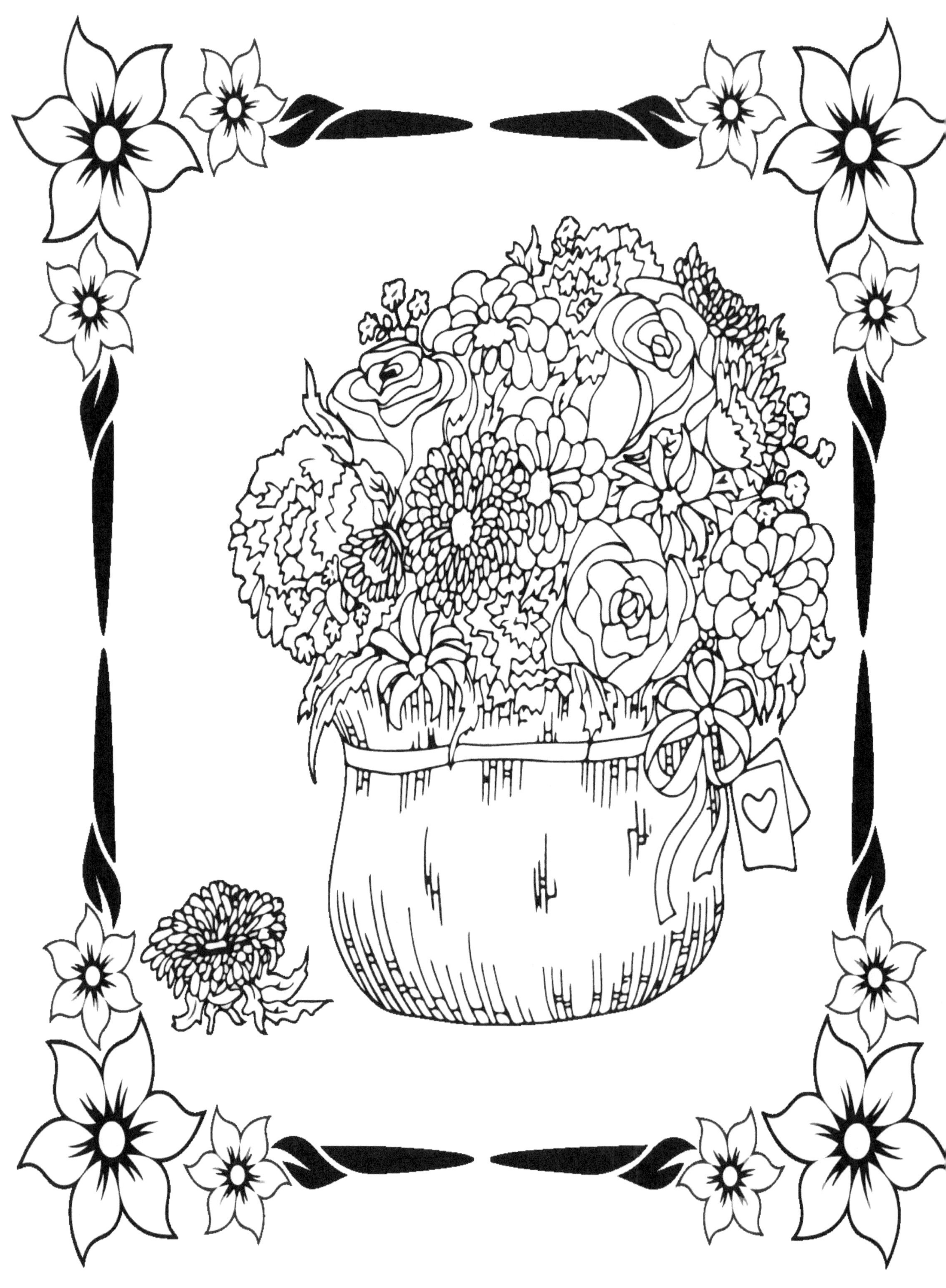

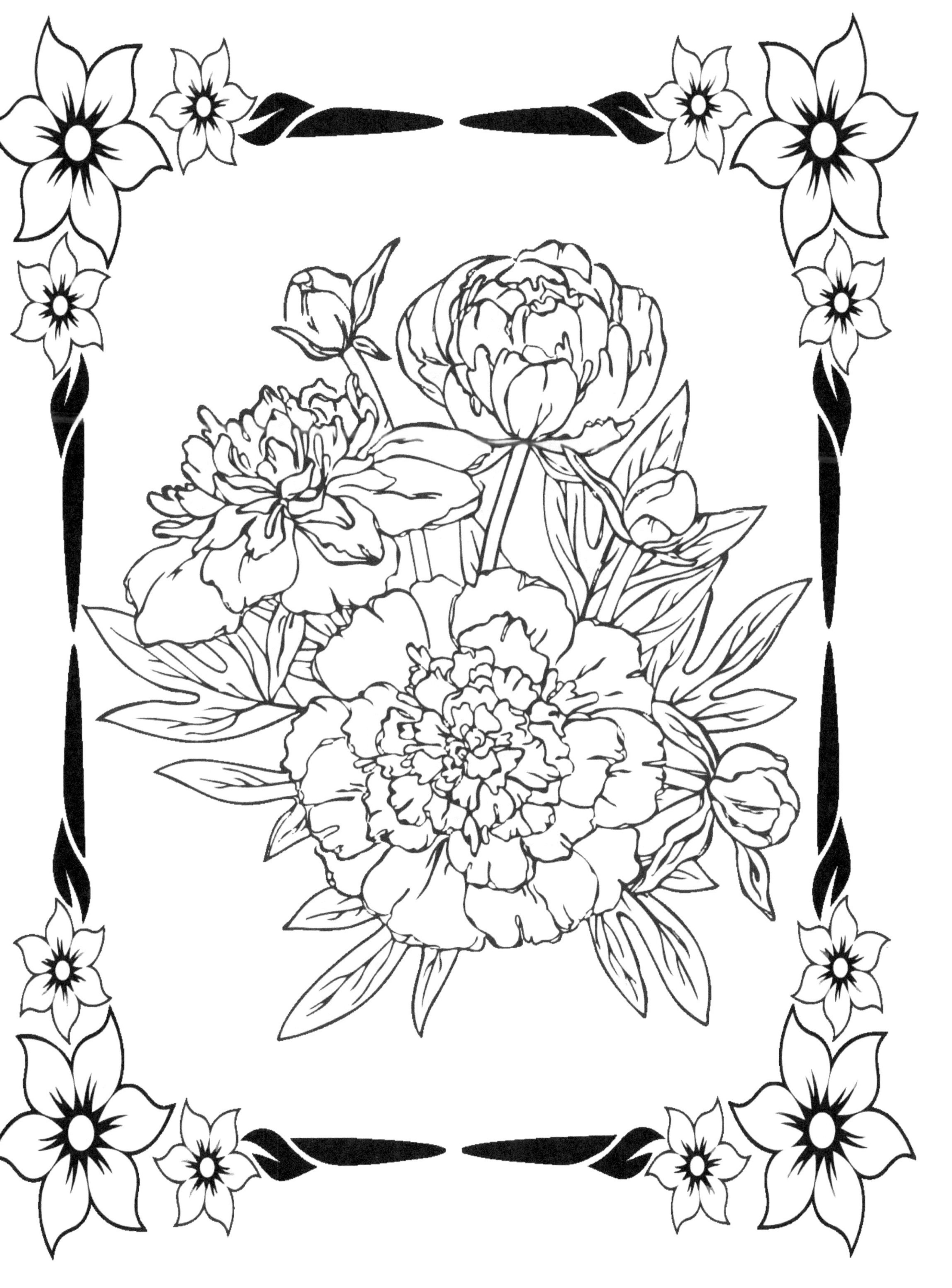

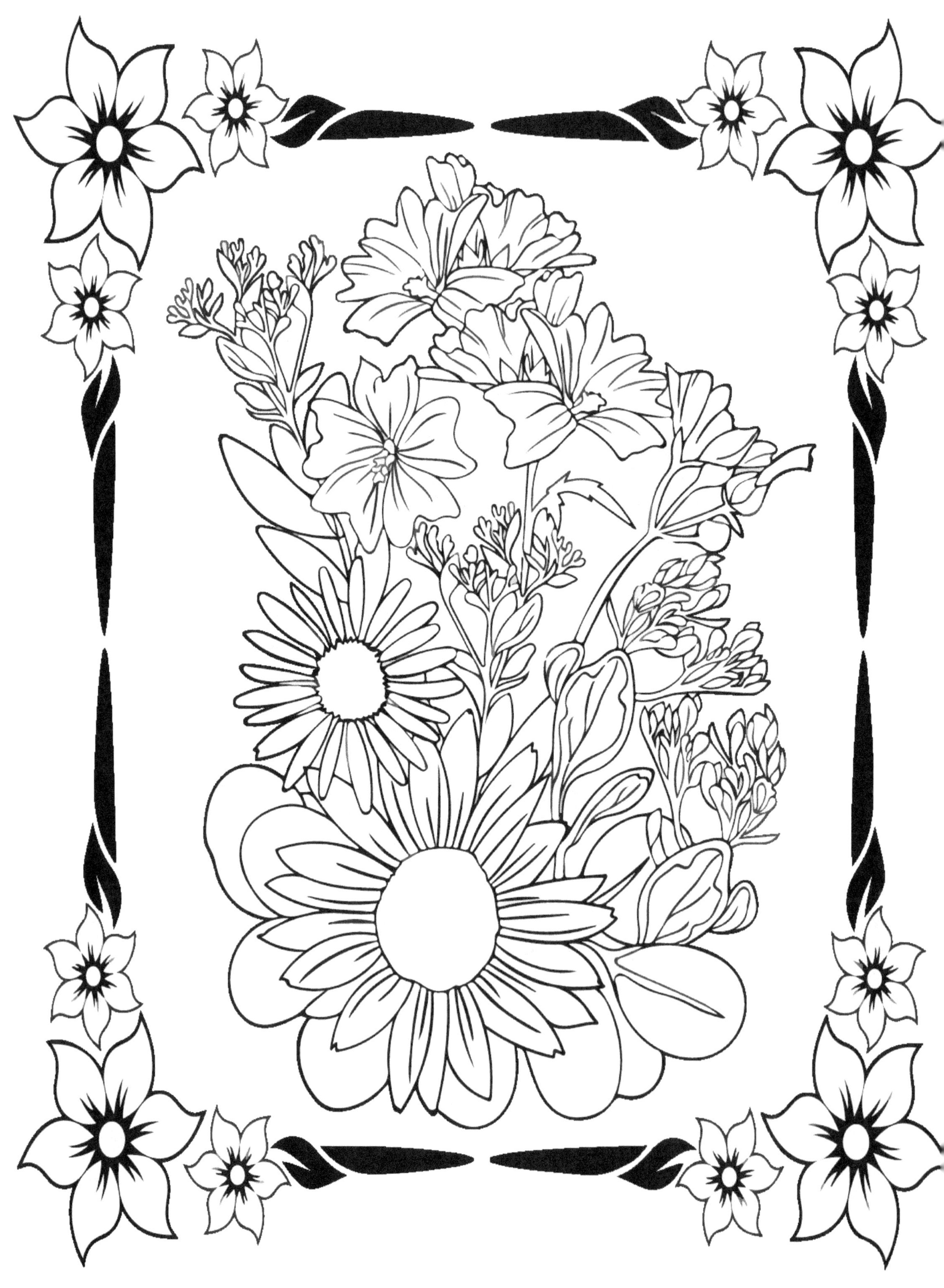

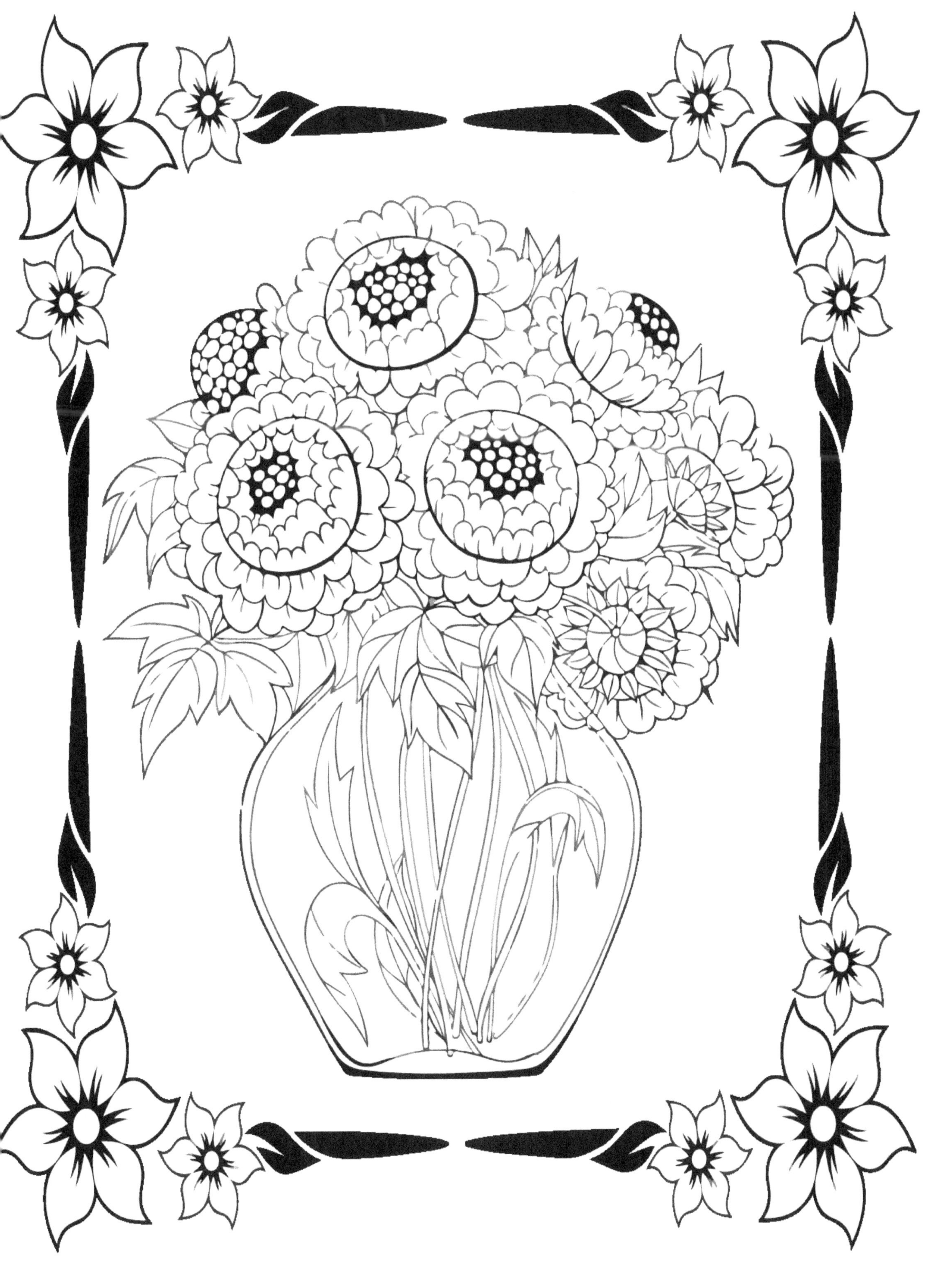

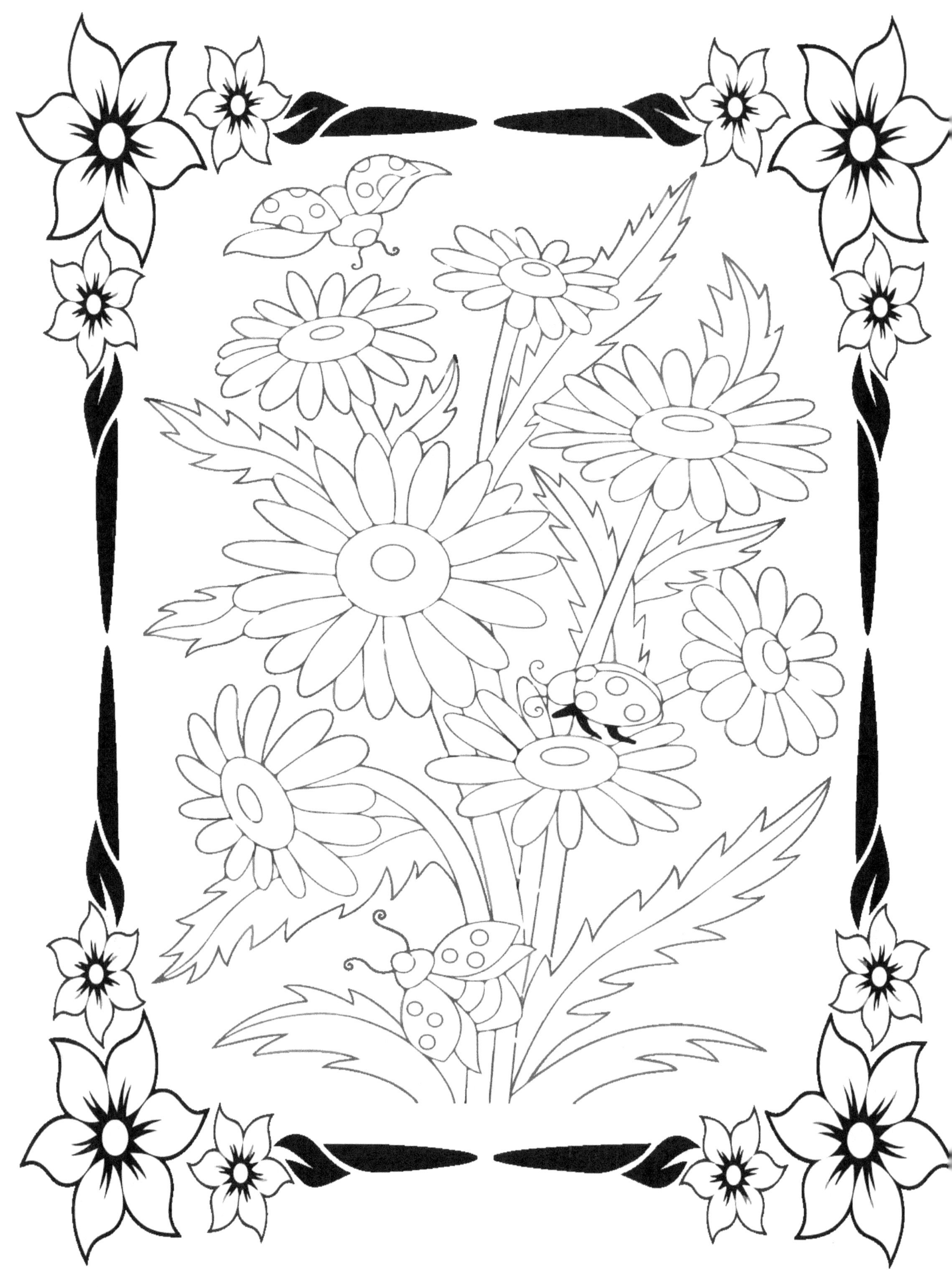

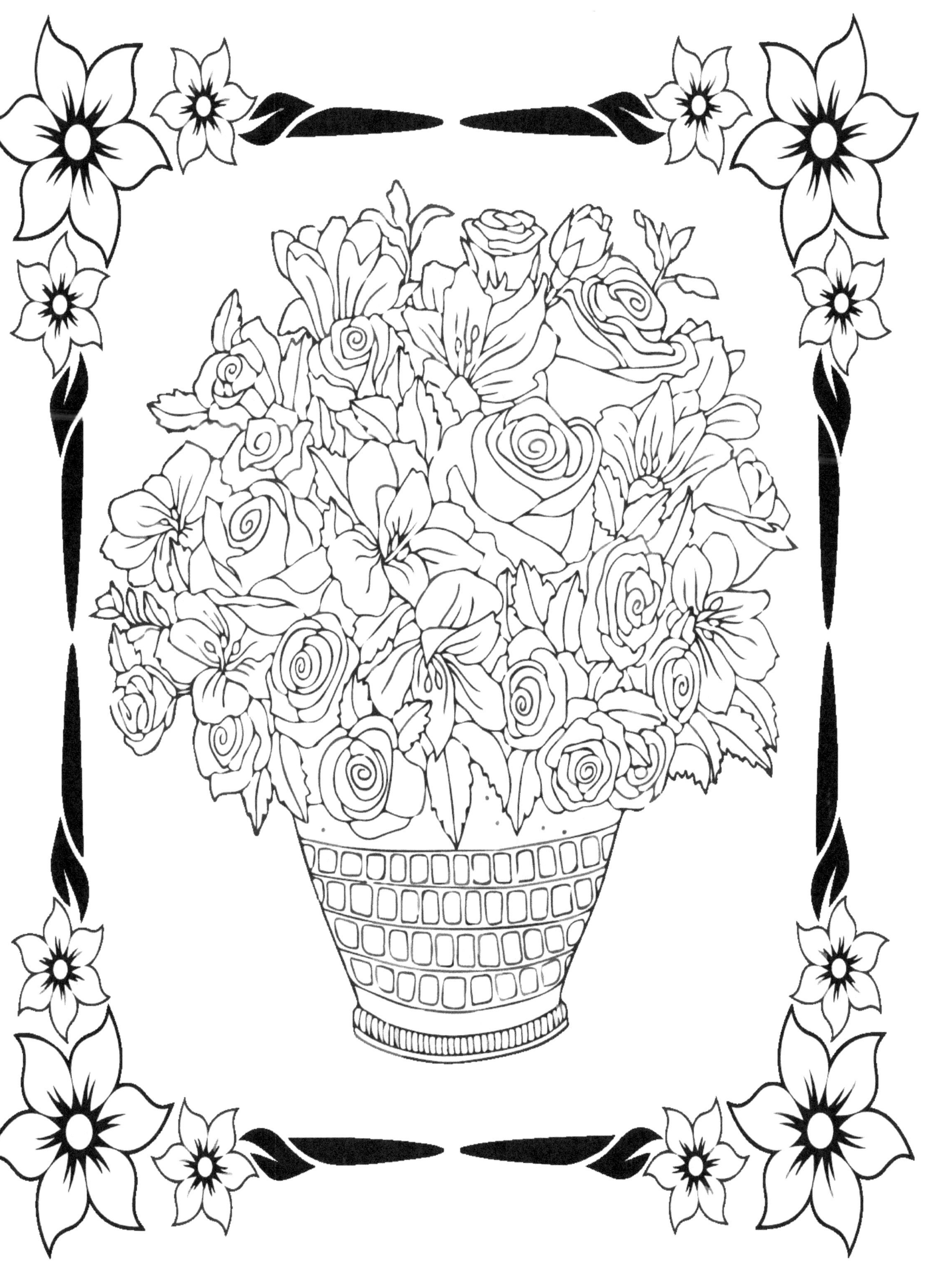

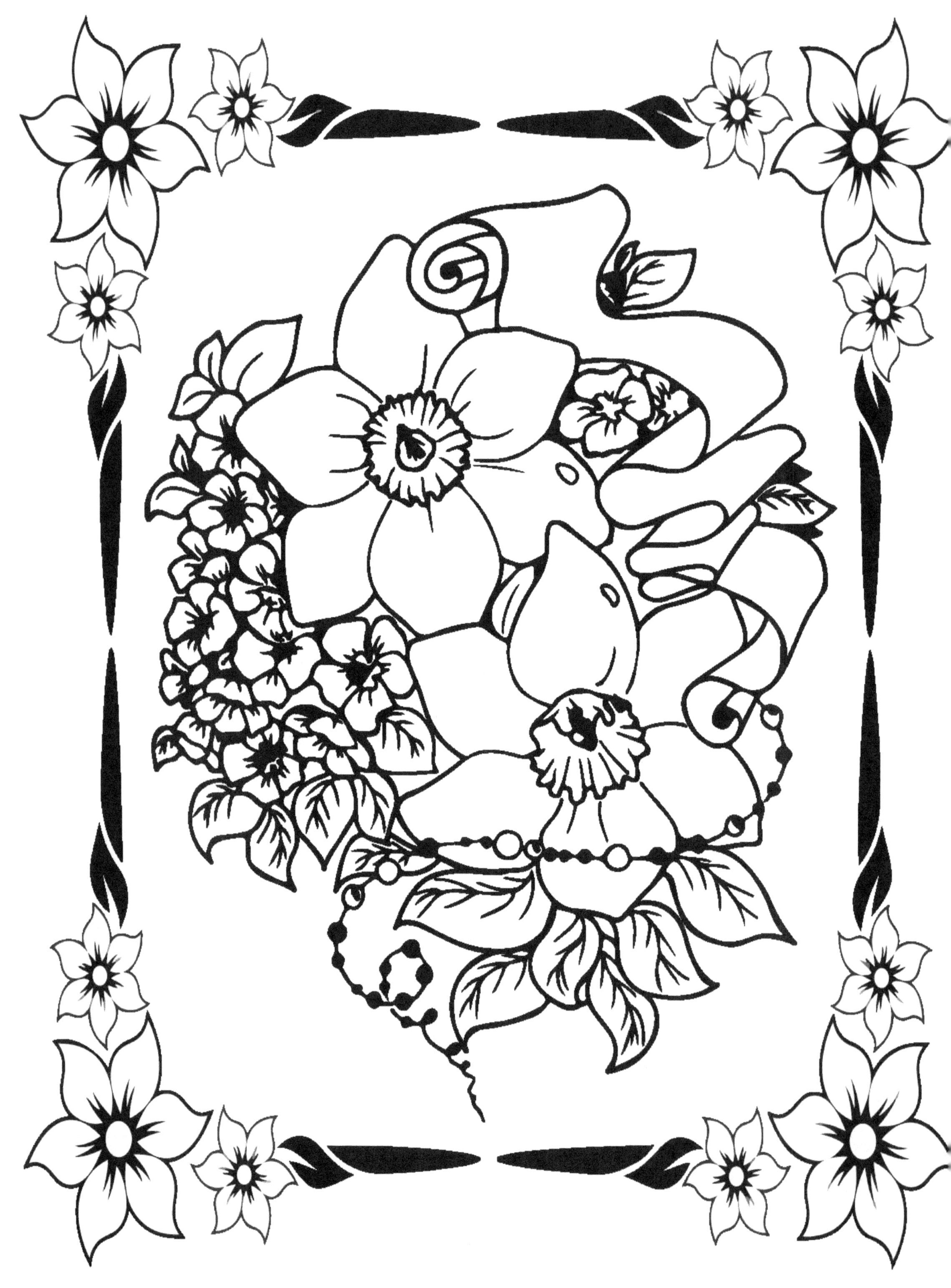

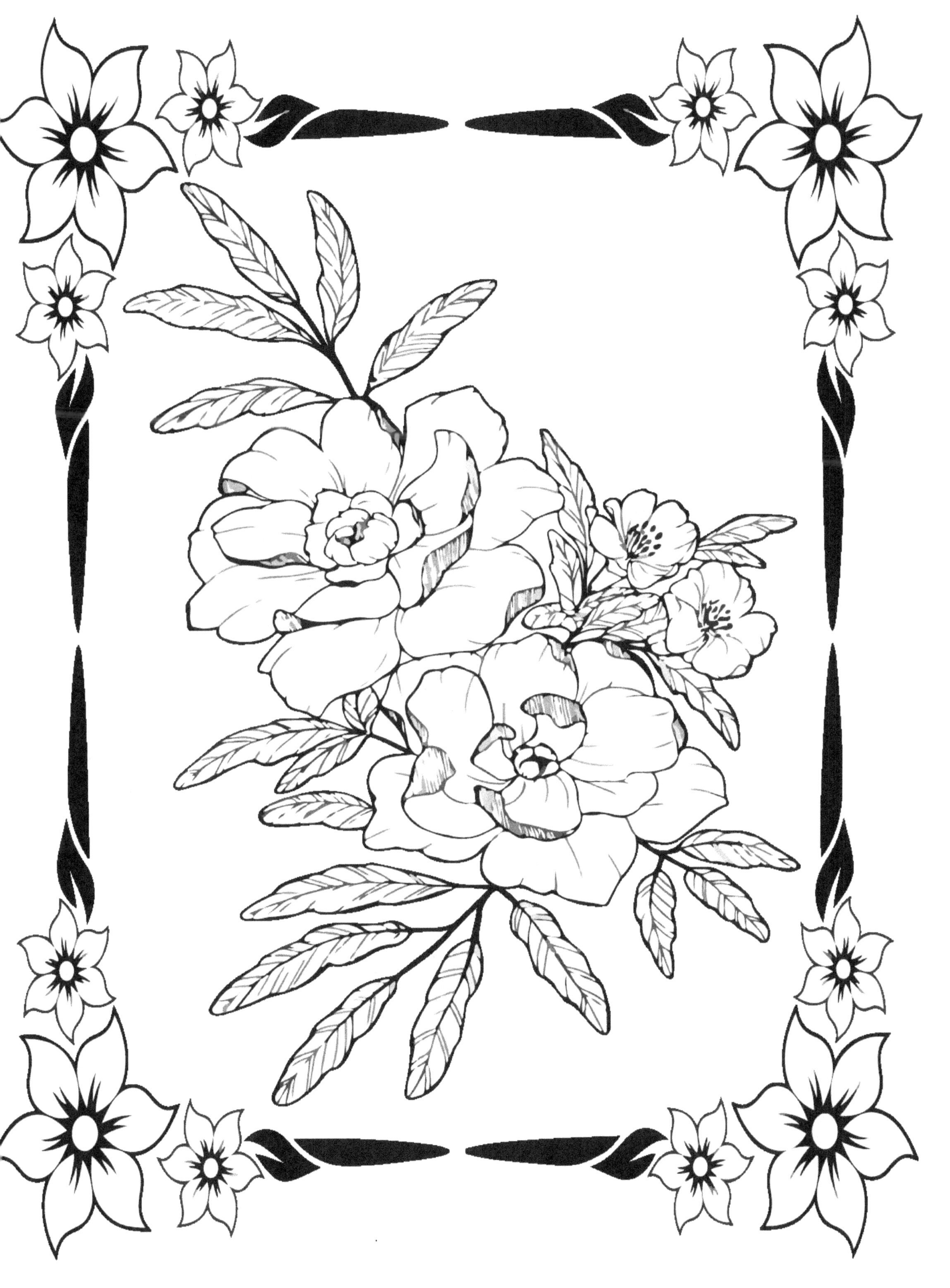

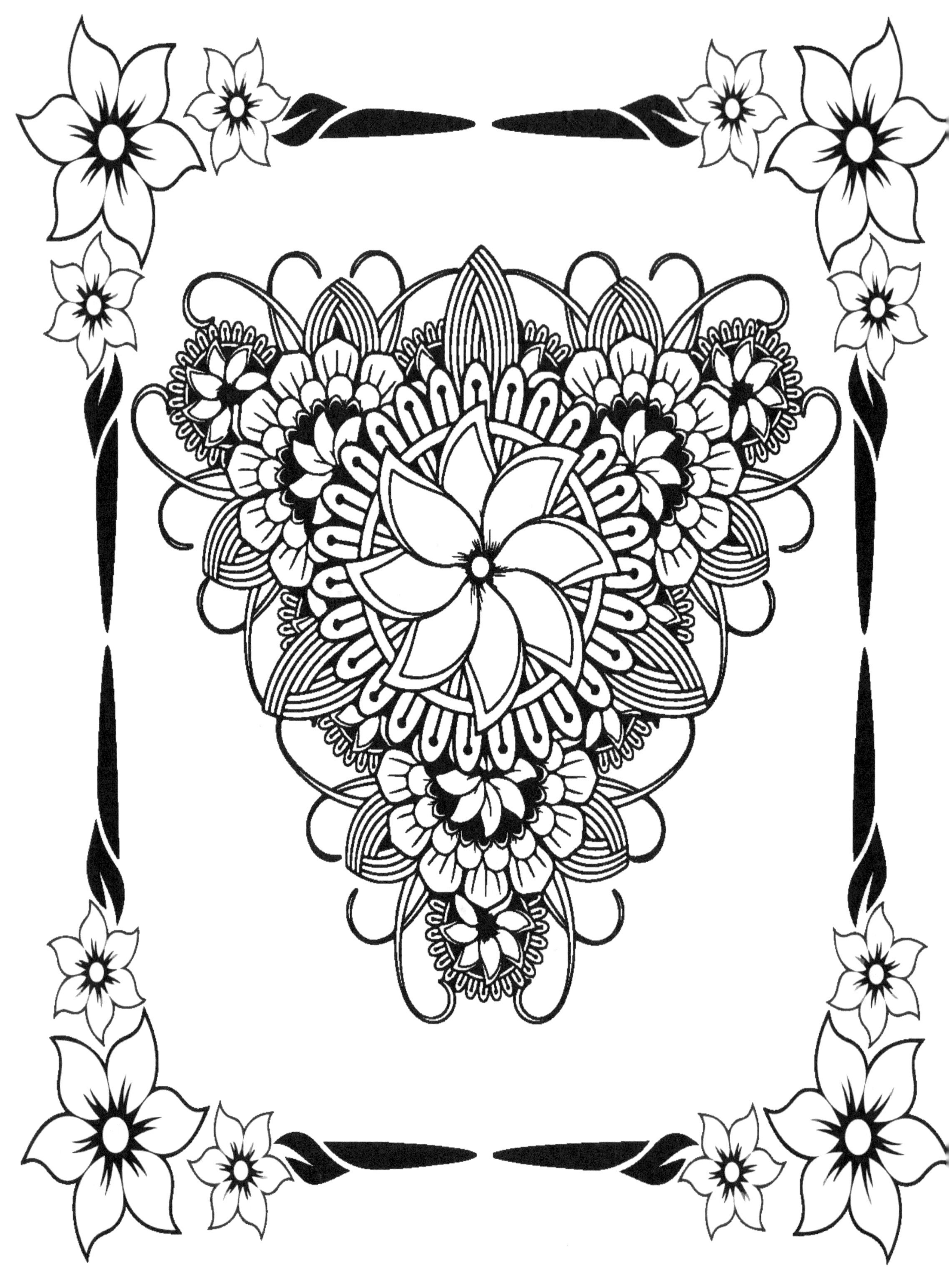

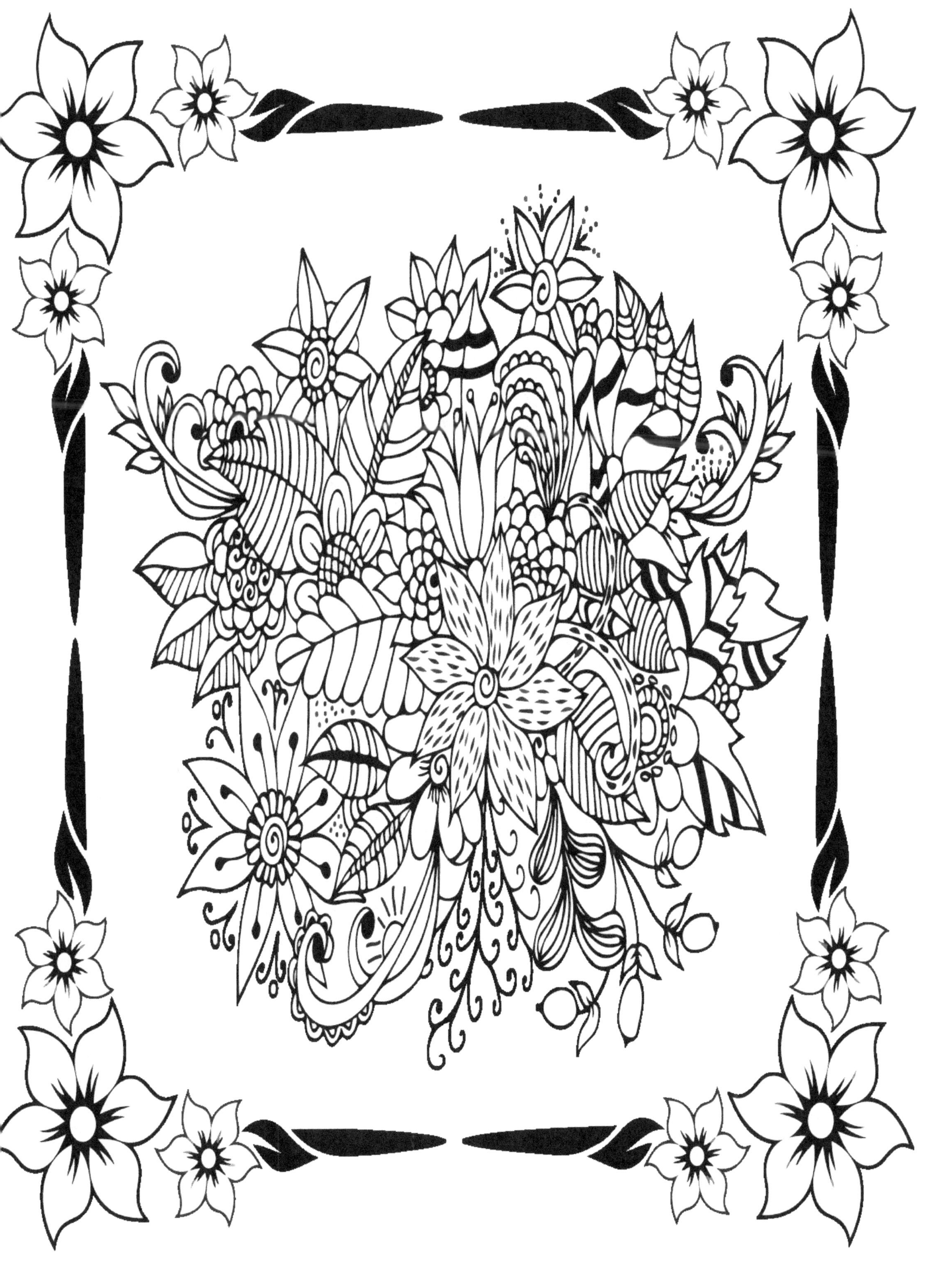

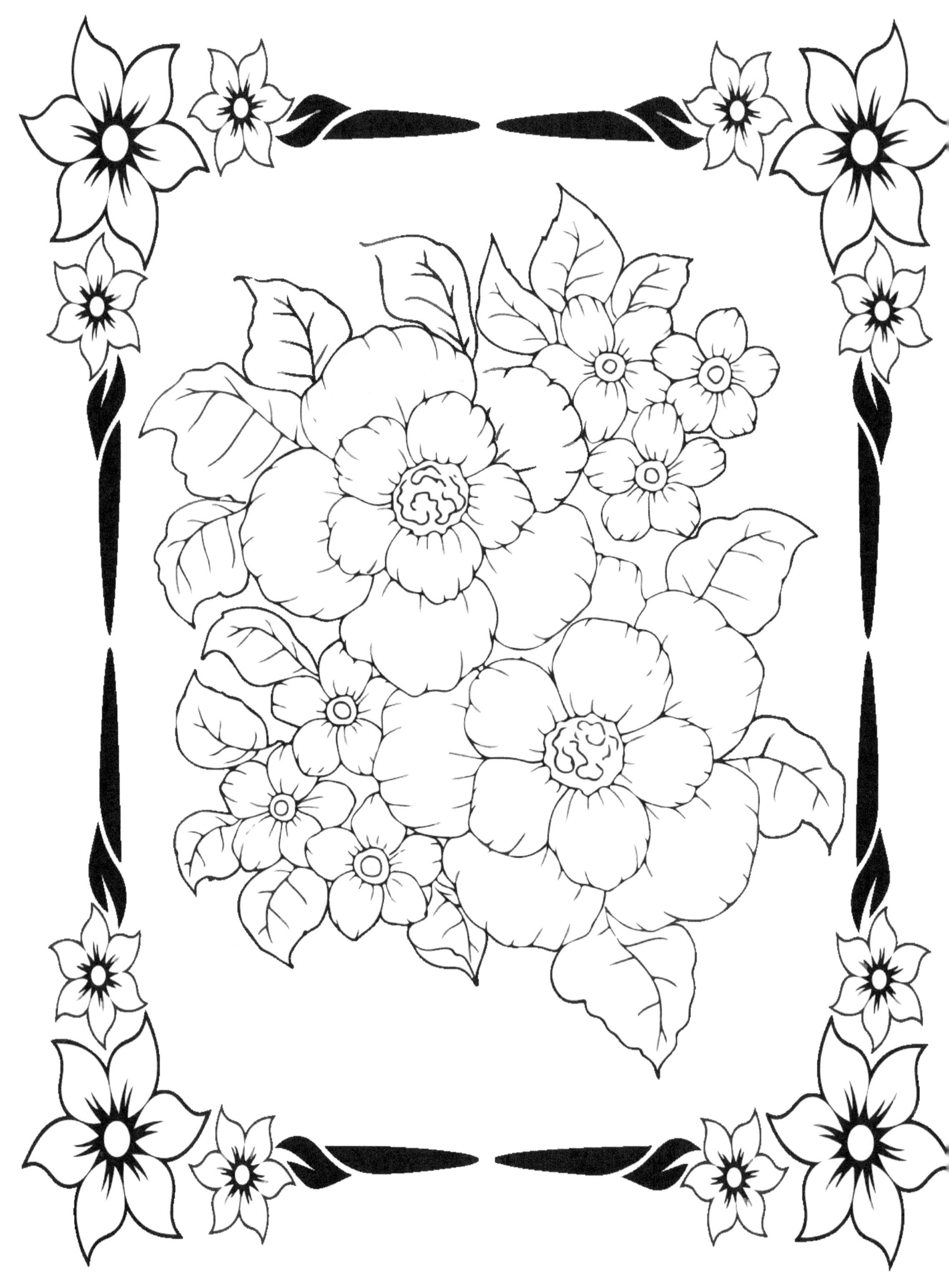

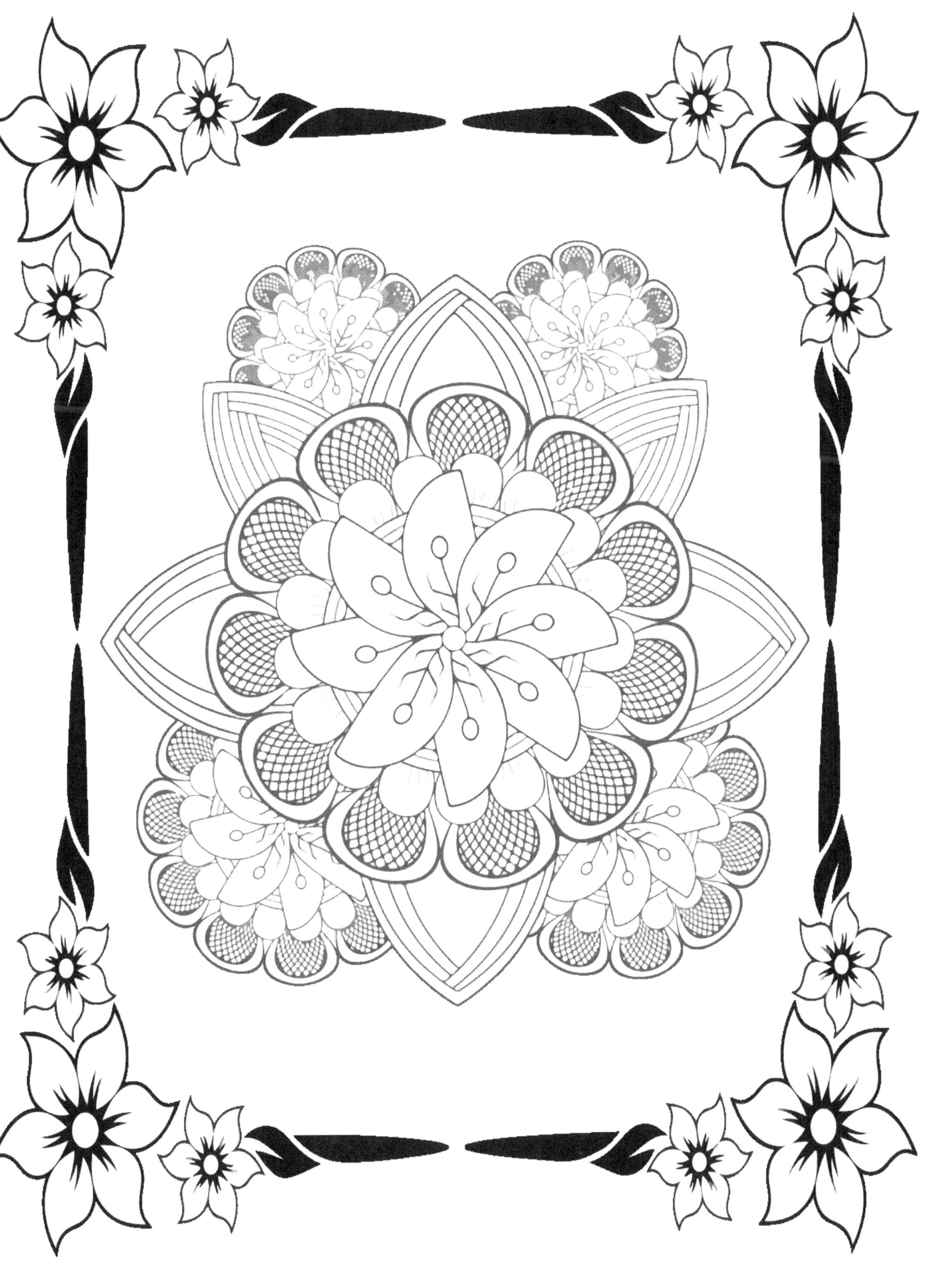

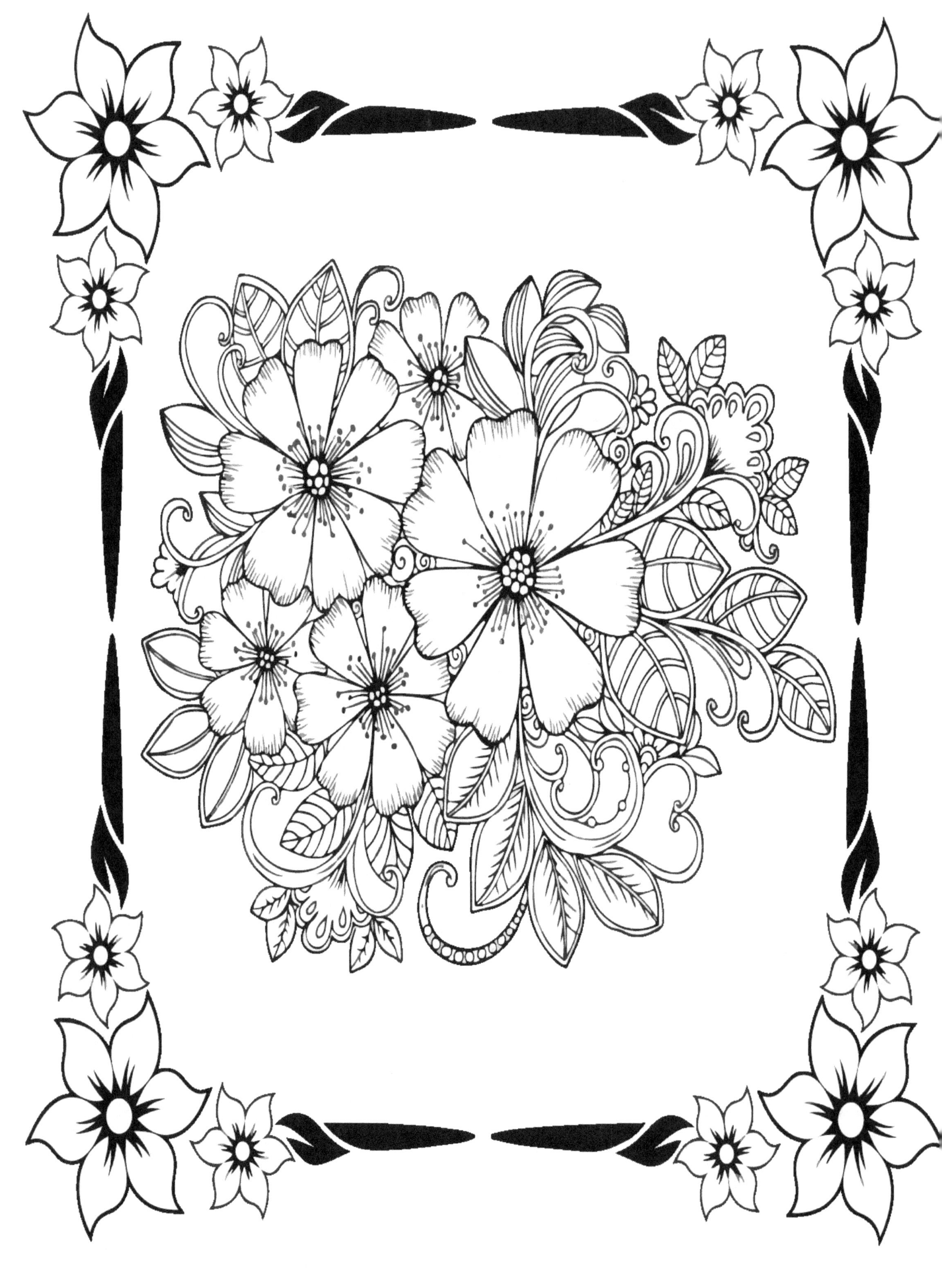

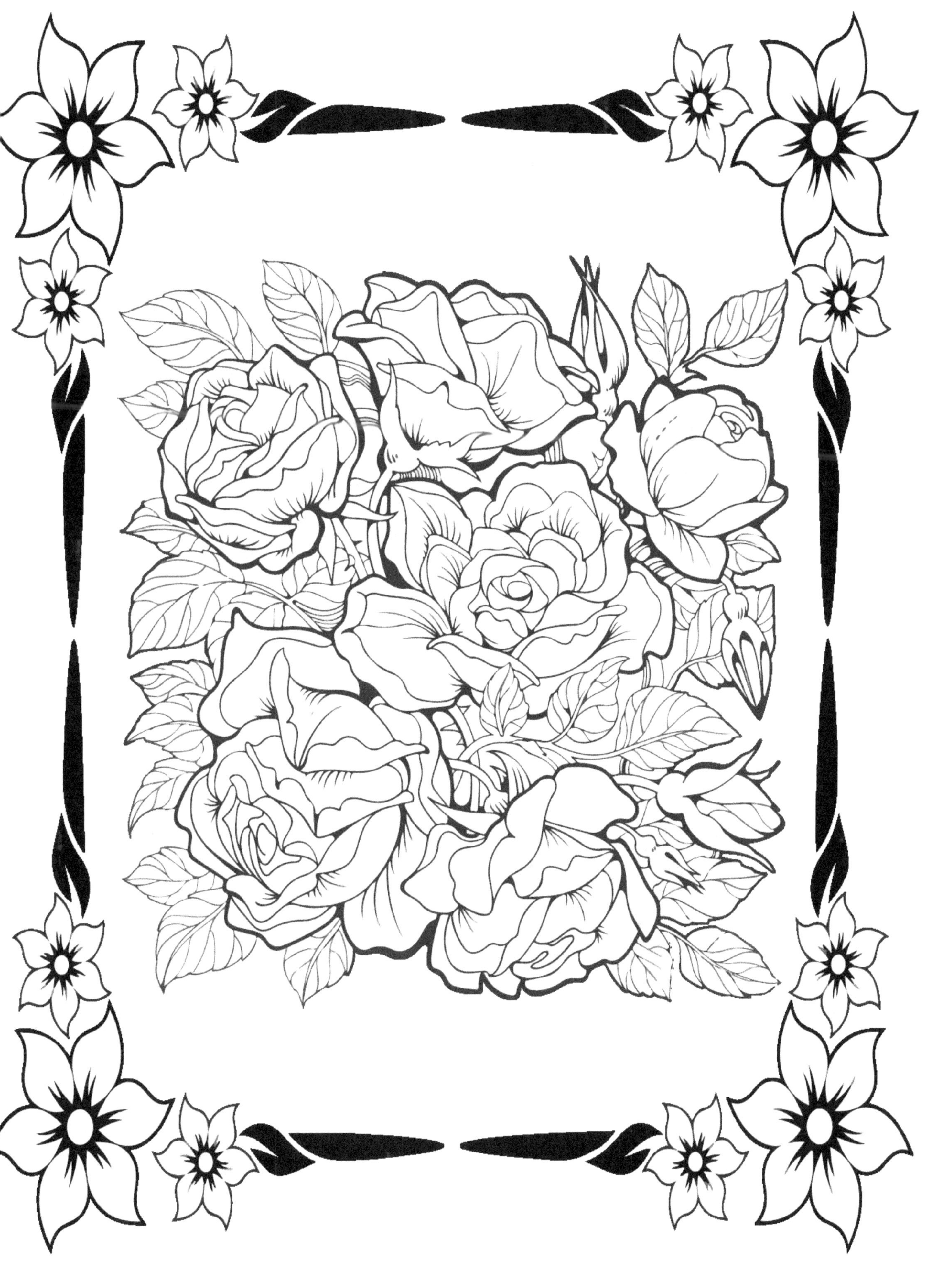

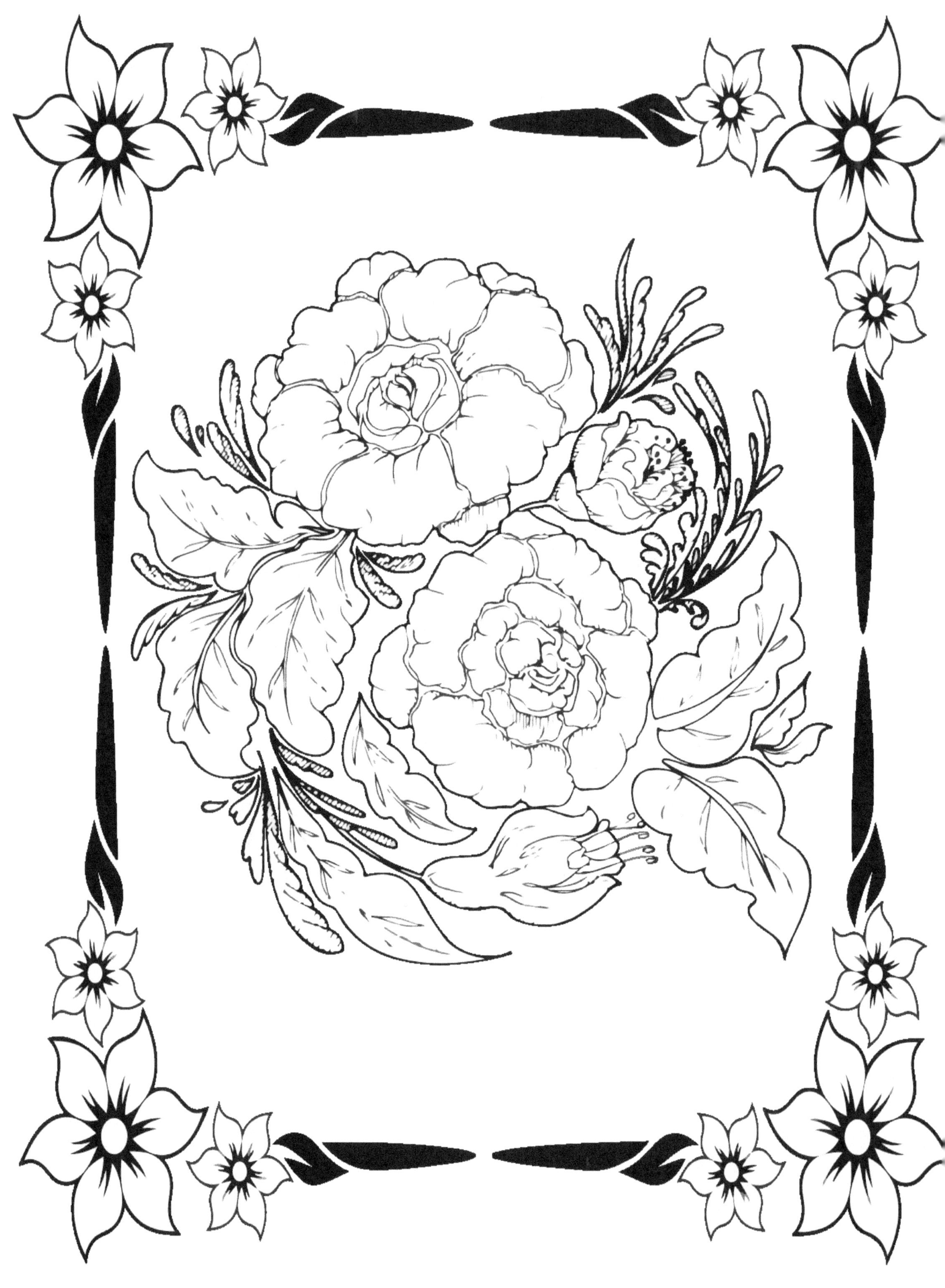

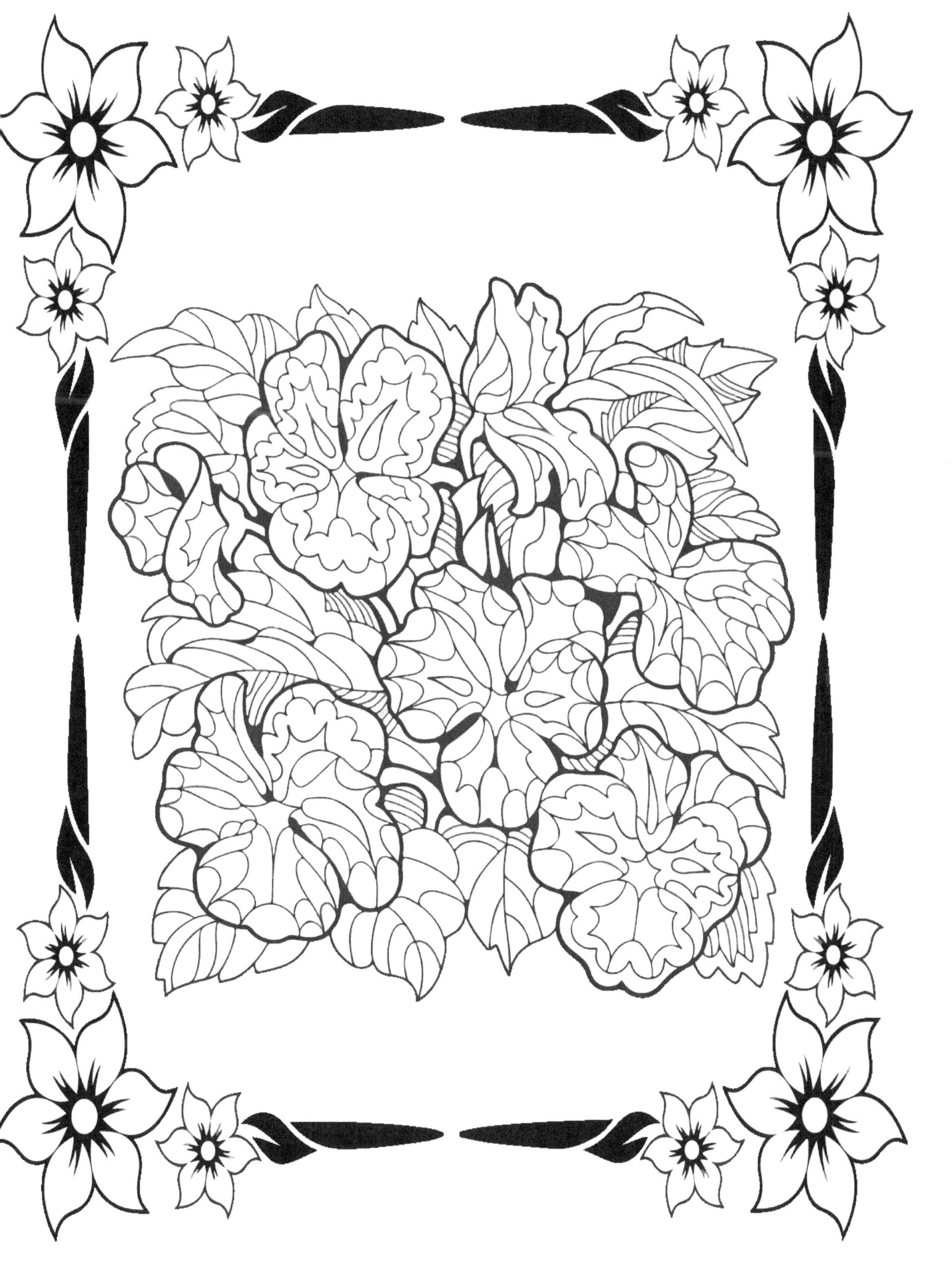

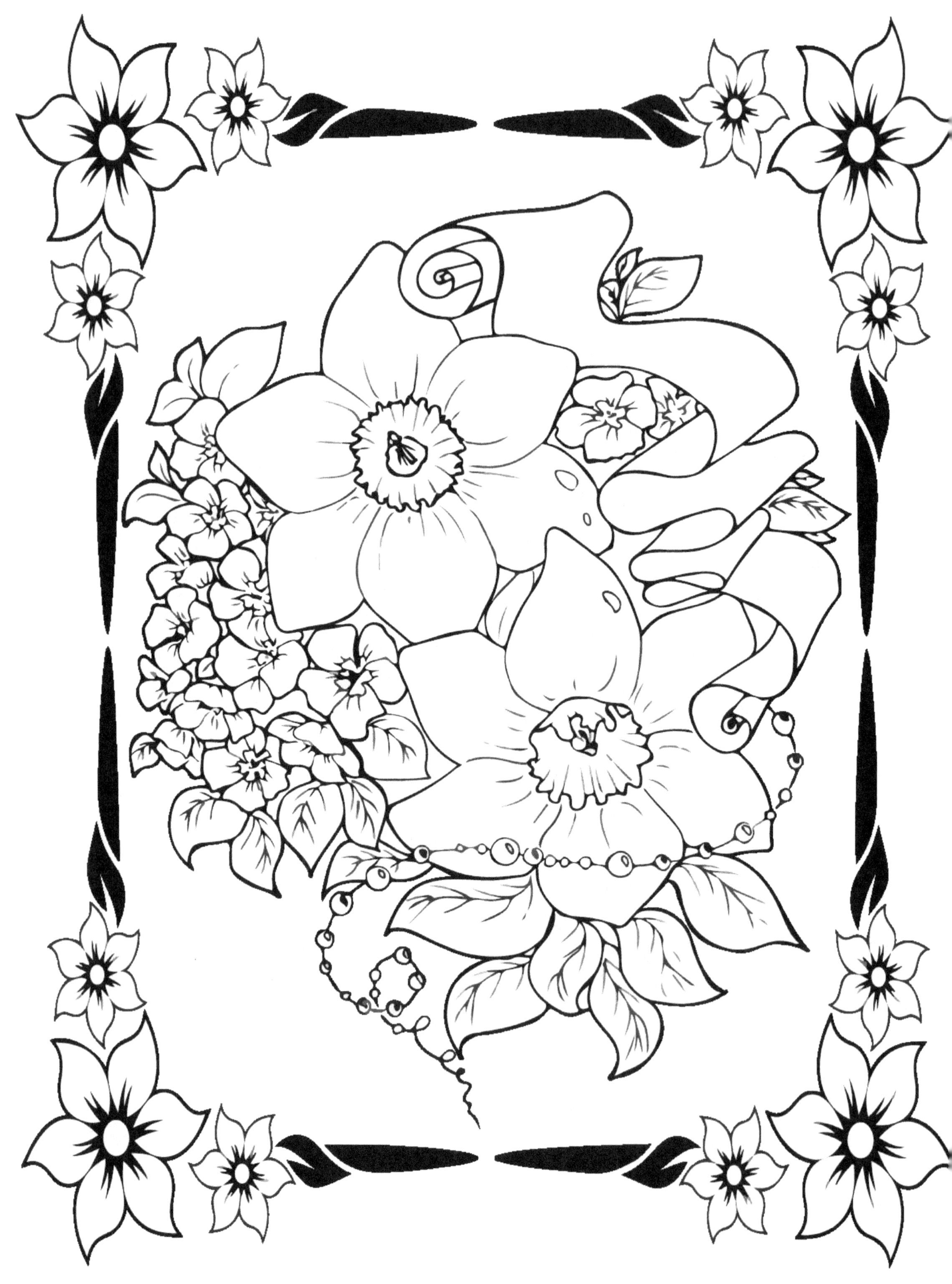

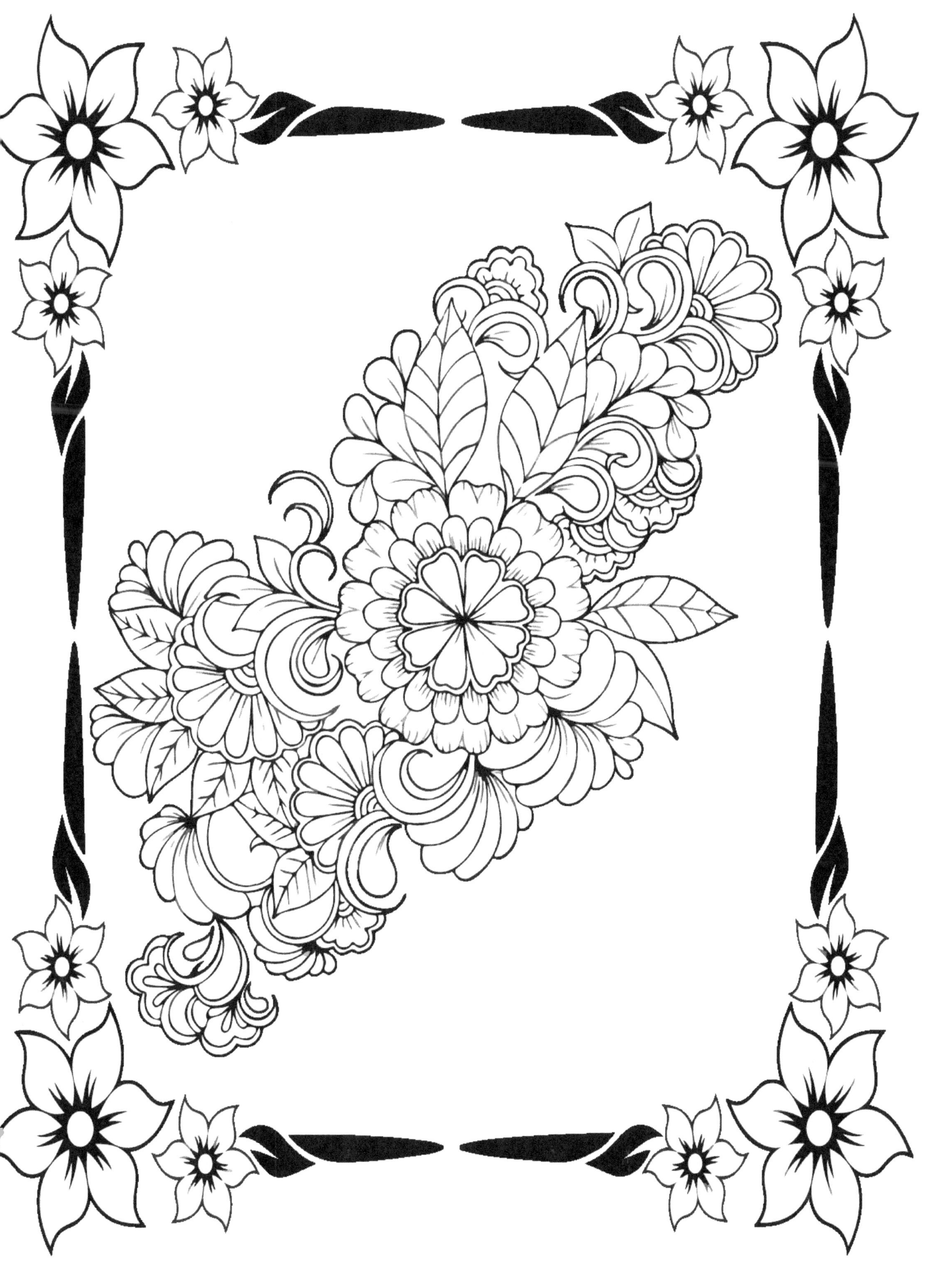

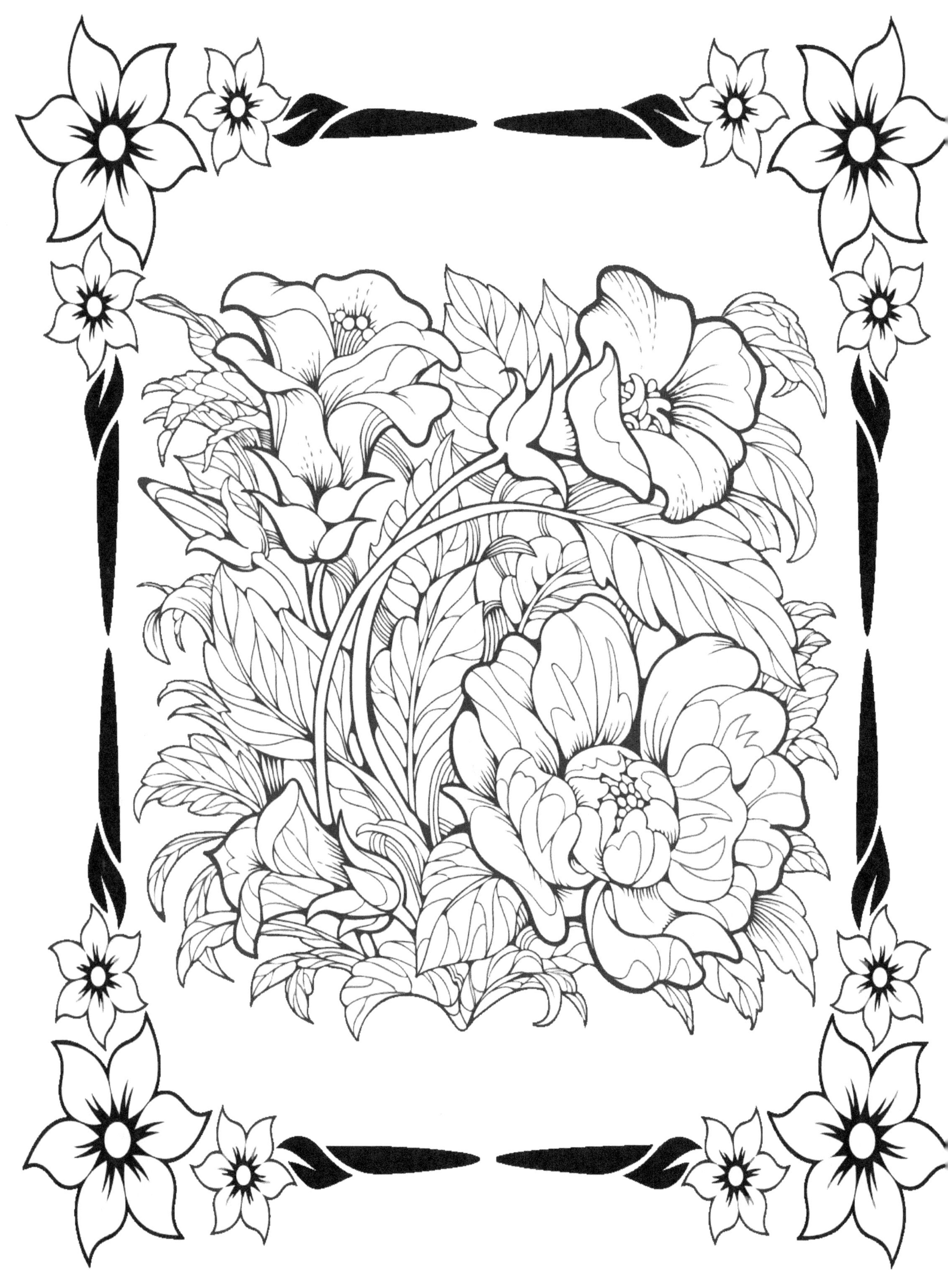

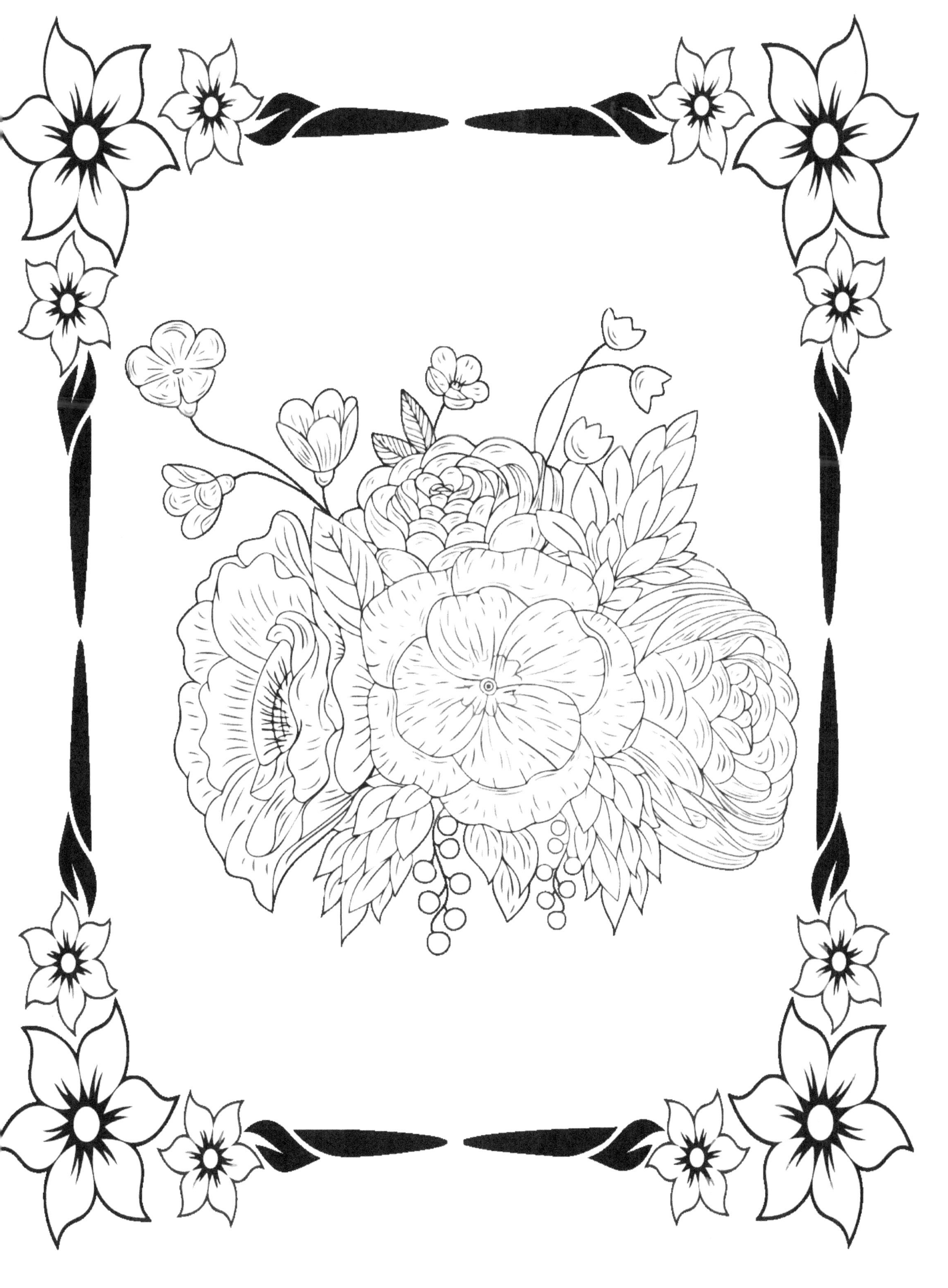

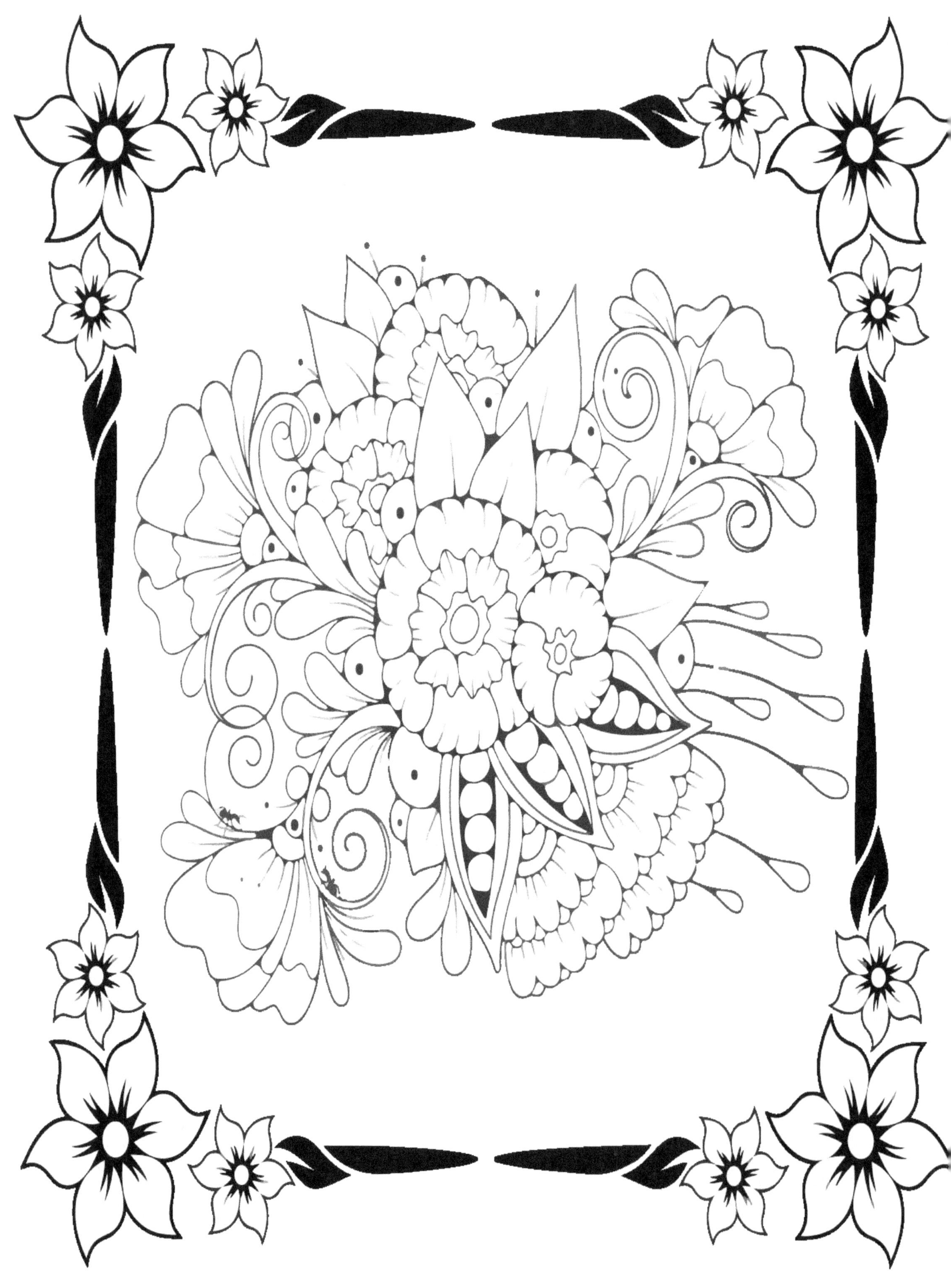

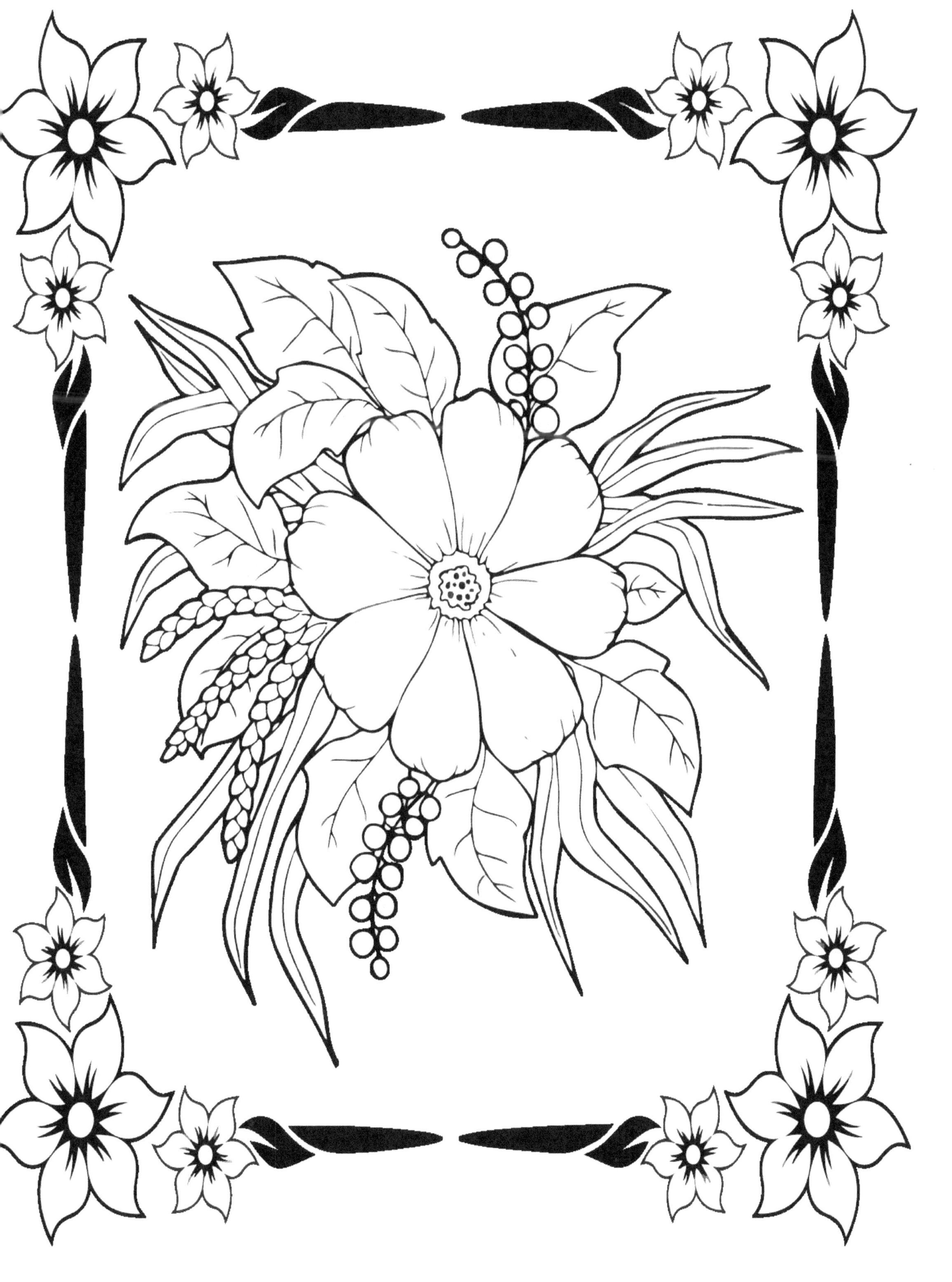

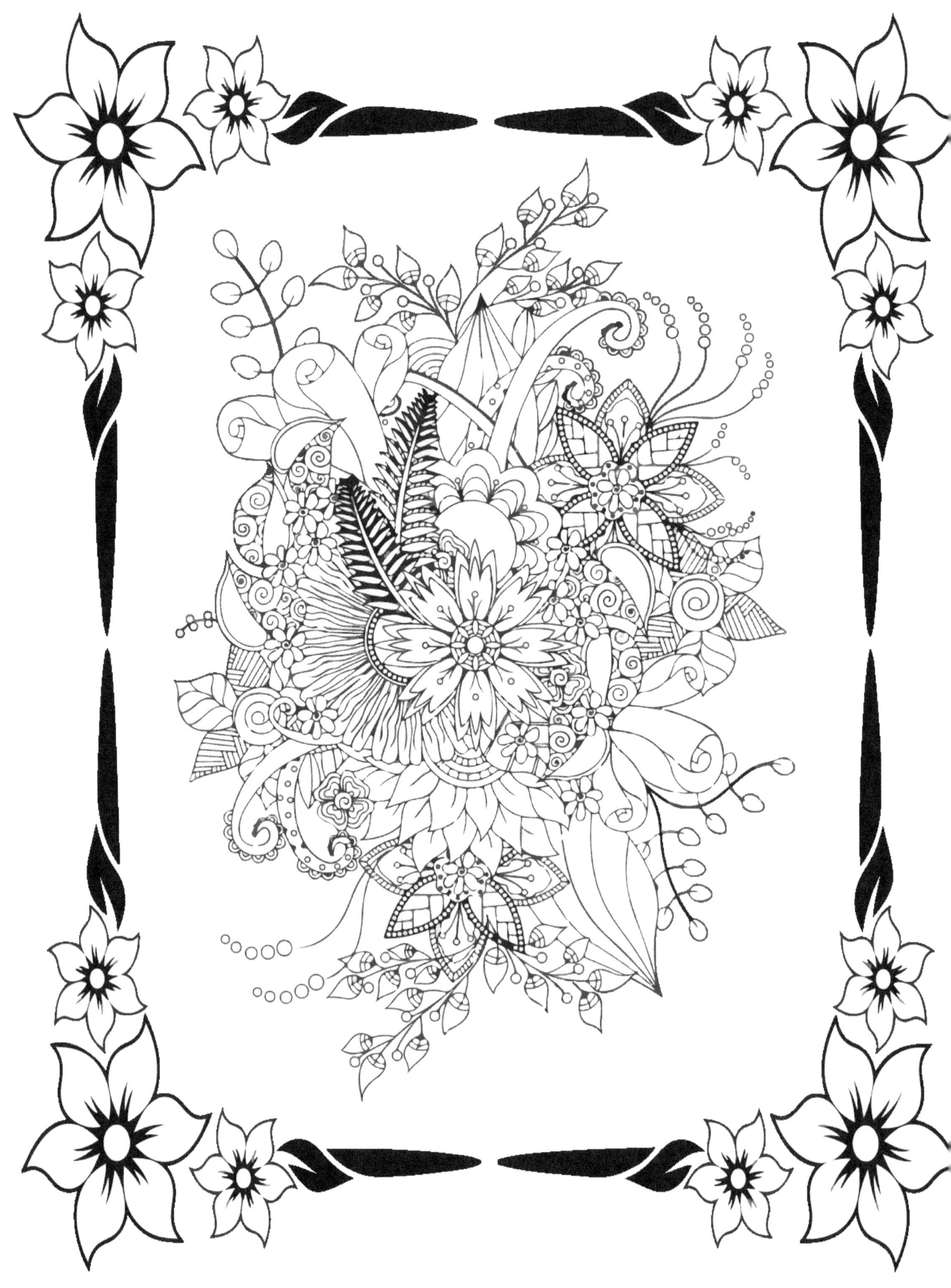

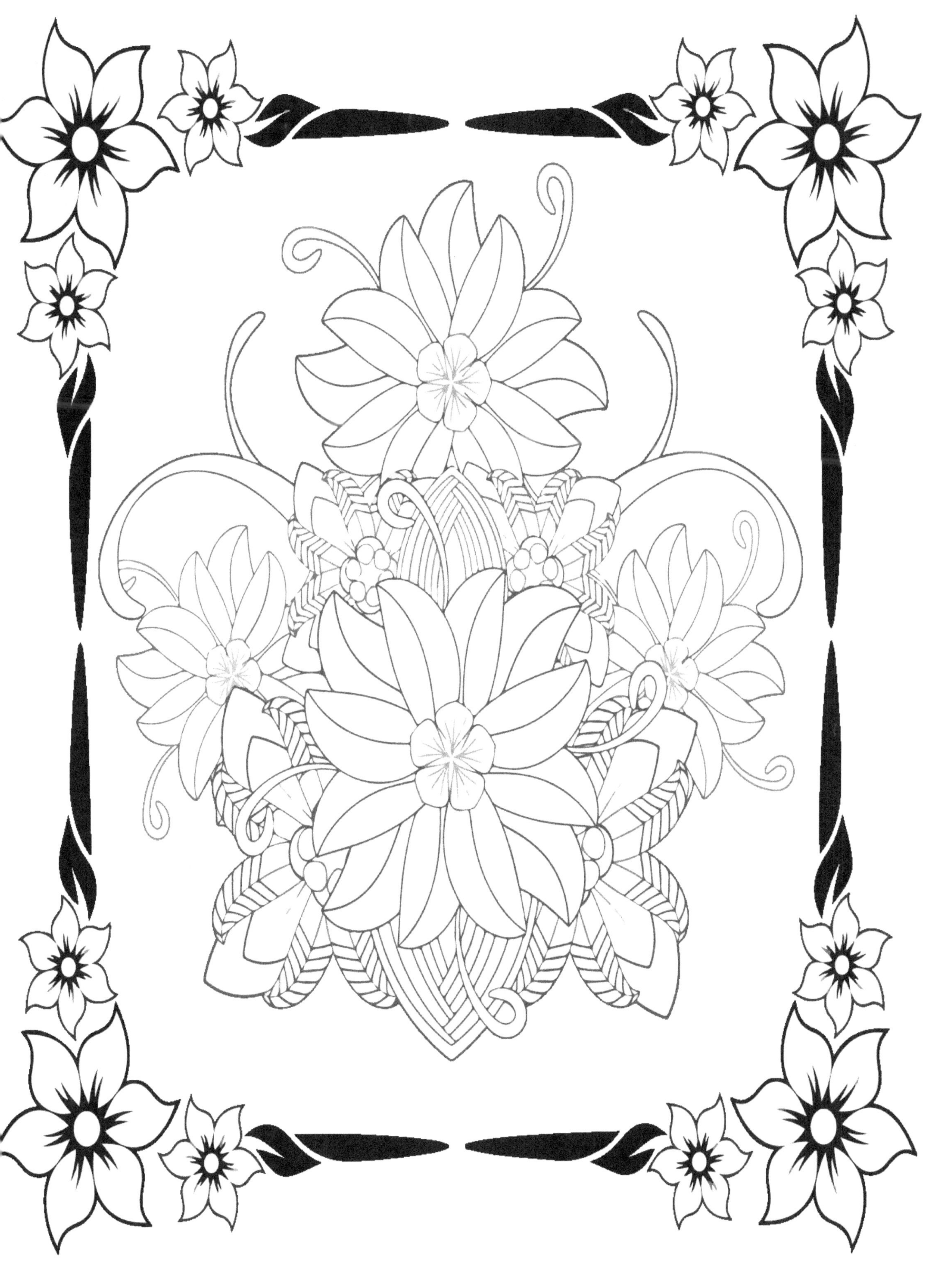

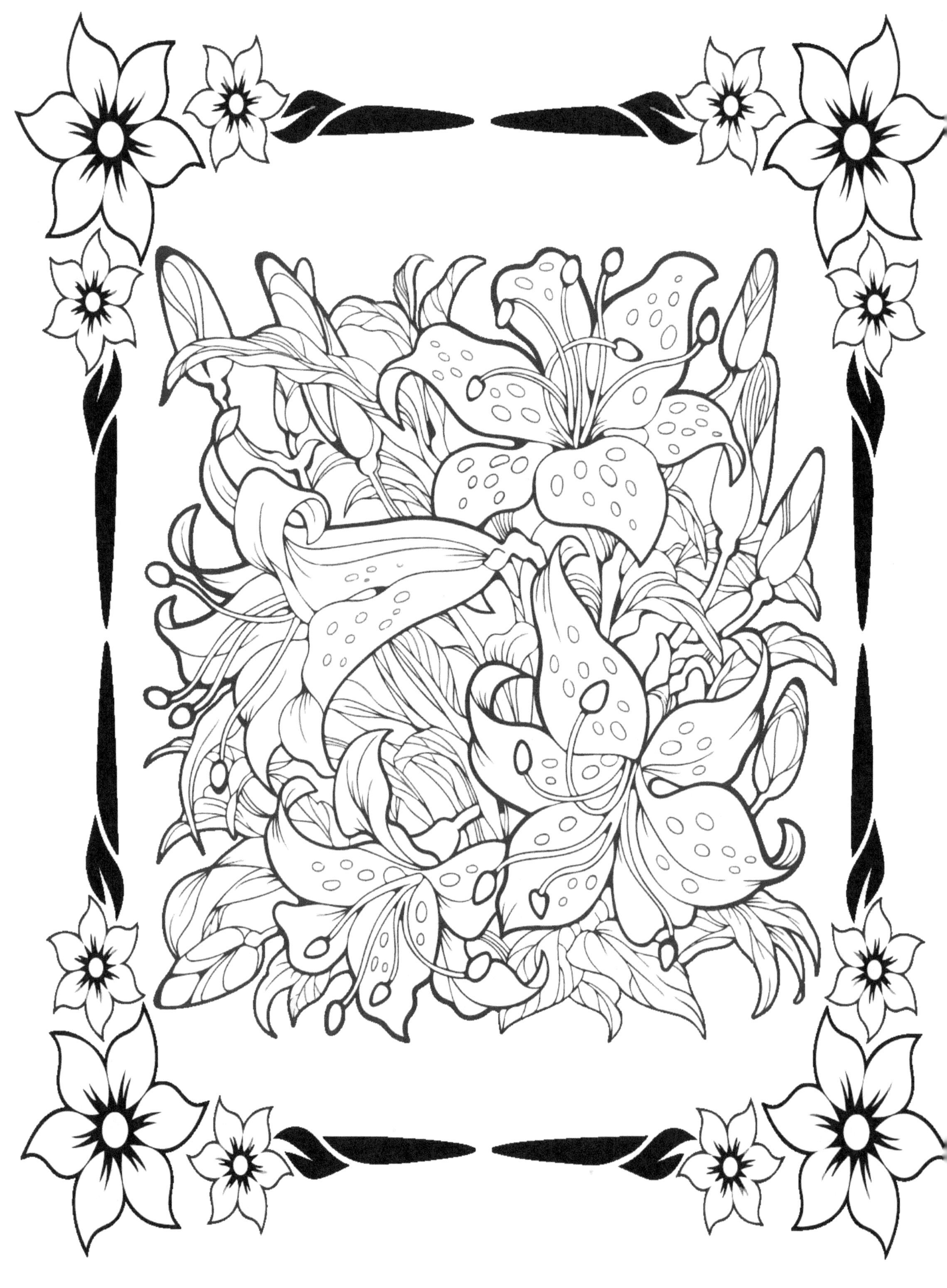